Bloody Mary in the Mirror

Bloody Mary in the Mirror
ESSAYS IN PSYCHOANALYTIC FOLKLORISTICS

Alan Dundes

University Press of Mississippi   Jackson

www.upress.state.ms.us

Copyright © 2002 by Alan Dundes
All rights reserved
Manufactured in the United States of America

Print-on-Demand Edition.

Library of Congress Cataloging-in-Publication Data

Dundes, Alan.
    Bloody Mary in the mirror : essays in psychoanalytic folkloristics / Alan Dundes.
      p. cm.
    Includes bibliographical references and index.
    ISBN: 978-1-60473-187-3
      1. Psychoanalysis and folklore. 2. Folklore—Classification. I. Title.

GR42 .D854 2002
398'.01'9—dc21   2002020837

British Library Cataloging-in-Publication Data available

CONTENTS

Preface vii

Acknowledgments xix

1. The Psychoanalytic Study of Religious Custom and Belief:
   Ritual Fasting, Self-Mutilation, and the *Deus Otiosus* 3

2. The Vampire as Bloodthirsty Revenant:
   A Psychoanalytic Post Mortem 16

3. Projective Inversion in the Ancient Egyptian "Tale of Two Brothers" 33

4. The Trident and the Fork:
   Disney's "The Little Mermaid" as a Male Construction of an Electral Fantasy
   (*with Lauren Dundes*) 55

5. Bloody Mary in the Mirror:
   A Ritual Reflection of Pre-Pubescent Anxiety 76

6. The Elephant Walk and Other Amazing Hazing:
   Male Fraternity Initiation through Infantilization and Feminization
   (*with Lauren Dundes*) 95

7. The Greek Game of *Makria Yaidoura* [Long Donkey]:
   An Adolescent Articulation of a Mediterranean Model of Masculinity 122

Epilogue 137

Index 139

PREFACE

Folkloristics is the study of folklore, much as linguistics is the study of language. The discipline of folkloristics may be said to have begun with the writings of Herder, who coined the term "Volkslied" [folksong] in 1773, and the celebrated publications of the brothers Grimm, whose famous two volumes of folktales, *Kinder-und Hausmärchen,* were published in 1812 and 1815 respectively. (For a better sense of the history of folklore scholarship, see Cocchiara 1981 and Dundes 1999.)

Of course, there were individuals before Herder who were fascinated by myths, folktales, legends, folksongs, proverbs, riddles, curses, charms, superstitions, and children's games, among many other folklore genres, but it is safe to say that folkloristics as a serious academic discipline became established in Europe only in the nineteenth century. The first true professorship in folkloristics was occupied by Norwegian folklorist Moltke Moe at the University of Oslo in 1886. The prestigious international folklore monograph series, the Folklore Fellows Communications, began publication in 1907. The first doctorate in folklore in the United States was awarded in 1953 by Indiana University to Warren Roberts, whose dissertation was a comprehensive comparative study of some nine hundred versions of the fairy tale of the Kind and Unkind Girls, Aarne/Thompson tale type 480 (Roberts 1994). From these few details, one can see that though the subject matter of folklore is presumably as old as mankind itself, the formal study of folklore as such has existed for just two centuries.

There are folklorists all over the world who work mostly within national or regional parameters. They assiduously collect local traditions from talented informants, resulting in hundreds of published volumes of folktales or customs and the like. Within the ranks of these folklorists is a small handful who are internationally minded. Inasmuch as folklore does not respect manmade political borders, one can usually find a given myth or children's game in many different cultures. It has been these international folklorists such as Kaarle Krohn and Antti Aarne of Finland, Axel Olrik and Bengt Holbek of Denmark, Carl Wilhelm von Sydow of Sweden, Johannes Bolte of Germany, Giuseppe Pitrè of Italy, James George Frazer of England, among others, who have studied a particular item of folklore wherever in the world it is found. (For details about these folklorists, see Dundes 1999.) But these are the exceptions, as most folklorists, who may lack the polyglot expertise required for such study, are usually perfectly content to concentrate exclusively on the local traditions immediately available in their own home area and transmitted in their own native language. The association of the interest in folklore with feelings of nationalism or regional or ethnic pride is well known.

Although the vast majority of folklore scholarship tends to be descriptive, consisting largely if not entirely of texts, recorded from informants, there have been a series of theories proposed over the centuries designed to explain the apparently irrational and fantastic content of much of folklore. Magic wands or toothed vaginas or talking animals are clearly products of the human imagination and thereby require some sort of explanation. Unfortunately, most of the folklore theories have not been very helpful in elucidating these puzzling and enigmatic elements. One such theory, popular in the nineteenth century was "solar mythology." It was argued that primitive man's myths were translations of his descriptions of the rising and setting of the sun. (There was a competing theory of "lunar mythology" which substituted the moon for the sun.) Another speculative theory claimed that all myths were derived from rituals. Even if no rituals were actually reported, it was simply assumed that any given myth, defined as the spoken counterpart of ritual, must be a survival from an original ritual. This myth-ritual theory is still to be found in the twenty-first century (Ackerman 1991, Segal 1998).

Other folkloristic theories or methods tended to be more empirical. For example, the structural approach to folklore was based on the idea that folklore genres were highly patterned and that the underlying pattern or structure could be discerned and described. The Russian folklorist Vladimir Propp's pioneering 1928 *Morphology of the Folktale* would be a stellar example of this approach (Propp 1968). The problem, once again, is that Propp's sequence of thirty-one units of fairy tale plot action (units that he calls "functions") does not really explain the significance, if any, of the magical nature of the fairy tale genre. Propp, a myth-ritualist, claimed that the fairy tale structure must derive from a primitive ritual of some kind (1984:105–8). Even the comparative method, the most basic approach to folklore, had as its goal the reconstruction of a presumed or hypothetical ur-form or original form of a given item of folklore. Little or no attempt was made in comparative studies of folklore to explain why the item may have been created in the first place or why it continued to be transmitted by bearers of tradition. To put it another way, the "meaning" or "meanings" (plural) of folklore were not investigated to any great extent by folklorists.

To be perfectly fair, it must be said that the tellers of tales and the singers of songs were not always able to provide exegeses of their traditions, or, if they were, folklore collectors failed even to attempt to elicit such folk *explications de texte*. It was deemed sufficient to record texts faithfully, preferably verbatim, and then publish them. This is why we have hundreds of books of folktales and folksongs without any information as to who told these tales or sang these songs, to what audiences, and on what occasions. Above all, the collectors offered no clue as to what the folklore they presented might *mean*. The governing philosophy seemed to be encapsulated in Emerson's aphoristic gnomic gem claiming that "Beauty is its own excuse for being." Analysis, it was felt, would run the risk of spoiling the beauty. Accordingly, in this philosophy, folktales and folksongs are regarded solely as ingenious works of verbal art of the highest order. It was deemed enough simply to enjoy a tale well told or a folksong artfully sung. One result of this longstanding failure to interpret folklore is the relative lack of respect that folklorists find in the academy. Folklorists are too often regarded (rightly, I think) by their fellow academics as mere collectors and classifiers, but rarely if ever as bona fide scholars seeking to analyze their data meaningfully.

Inasmuch as a large portion of folklore consists of fantasy material, it would seem obvious that the meaning(s) of such material cannot possibly be elucidated without recourse to some form of psychology. If we grant this, then the question arises as to what form of psychology should be employed. My own bias is that psychoanalysis provides the tools necessary for the illumination of folklore. Unfortunately, there is a strong feeling of unease and distrust among conventional folklorists (and most academics) whenever psychoanalysis is mentioned. Among historians, for example, the subfield known as "psychohistory" is not held in good repute. Psychohistory has as its premise that important acts in history carried out by individuals might possibly be influenced by the psychological factors affecting the personalities of those individuals. Similarly, psychoanalytic literary criticism is not universally popular in English and other literature departments. As for folklore, *psychoanalytic folkloristics* (the term is proposed here for the first time in this volume) can barely be said to exist at all.

Most of the attempts to apply psychoanalytic principles to folklore data have been made by psychoanalysts. Freud himself was much interested in folklore. His hobby of collecting Jewish jokes formed the basis of his *Wit and Humor in the Unconscious*, published in 1905. Freud also believed that the source of the symbols found in dreams came ultimately from folklore and furthermore that so-called Freudian symbolism was actually symbolism already previously articulated by the folk in their folklore. Freud was very clear about this: "How do we profess to arrive at the meaning of these dream-symbols, about which the dreamer himself can give us little or no information? My answer is that we derive our knowledge from widely different sources: from fairy tales and myths, jokes and witticisms, from folklore, i.e., from what we know of the manners and customs, sayings and songs, of different peoples, and from poetic and colloquial usage of language" (Freud 1953:166). Many of the members of Freud's early circle shared his interest in folklore. This includes Otto Rank, Carl Jung, and Ernest Jones, among others (Dundes 1985). Later psychoanalysts very much concerned with folklore were Bruno Bettelheim and especially Géza Róheim (cf. Róheim 1953, 1992, Ben-Amos 1994). The main problem with the psychoanalysts attempting to interpret folklore is that they were not really familiar with the range of folklore data and scholarship. Though hundreds of versions of a given folktale might be available, psychoanalysts invariably limited their "text" to just one, and it was invariably the one presented by the brothers Grimm, a text that in many instances represented a conflated synthetic combination of motifs from different German versions of the tale, a text, in short, that may never have been actually told in that form by any informant. In the tale of Hansel and Gretel (Aarne-Thompson tale type 327A), for example, it was the mother in the original oral tale that persuaded her husband to abandon the children in the woods. The Grimms, no doubt thinking it in the best interest of offering a more positive image of German culture, substituted "step-mother" in the fourth edition of their anthology. Psychoanalysts have generally tended to stick pretty close to the Grimm canon, leaving it only occasionally to consider classical myths and the Old Testament, hardly a representative sample of the overall richness of the world's folklore.

As for folklorists attempting to apply psychoanalytic principles to folklore, there are not many names one could list. Despite my best efforts over the past three decades, I seem to have failed to convince my colleagues or students of the utility of this approach. One well-meaning colleague went so far as to call me "a leader in the field without any followers!" I suspect that even my family members have wondered about my longstanding devotion to psychoanalytic folkloristics. For the record, I should like to say something about just how this came to be.

As a small boy growing up in a rural area near Patterson, New York, about sixty-five miles north of New York City, I was an avid reader. My parents encouraged me, not that any encouragement was really necessary, by offering me one dollar for every hundred books that I read. It didn't matter what these books were. I was free to choose whatever I liked. The only "rule," so to speak, was that I was supposed to keep a record of books read so that I could legitimately qualify for the one-dollar reward. I remember especially enjoying books of fairy tales. In fact, in my parents' home, which was filled with books, there was a multivolume series called *Journeys Through Bookland,* or at least that is my recollection of the title. In these volumes were interspersed fairy tales, and I recall thumbing through the pages of the various volumes in search of these tales. One anthology I very much enjoyed was *East of the Sun and West of the Moon.* At that time, I had no idea that this book, which remains to this day a standard staple of children's literature, was a famous translation by George Webbe Dasent of the important mid-nineteenth-century collection of Norwegian folktales made by Peter Christen Asbjörnsen (1812–1885) and Jörgen Moe (1813–1882), contemporaries of the Grimms. During my adolescent years, I particularly appreciated jokes of all kinds, many of which I much later discovered were contained in the late Gershon Legman's classic two volumes of *Rationale of the Dirty Joke,* which he analyzed from an unabashedly Freudian perspective.

But my childhood interest in fairy tales and jokes did not lead directly to a career as a psychoanalytic folklorist. There were two critical incidents that shaped my life, and I shall mention them if for no other reason than to demonstrate just how chance or luck can alter a person's world. The first incident occurred in 1952–53, my sophomore year at Yale. In the process of shifting from a music major to a major in English, I decided to take an elective course in psychology. I was very disappointed in the first semester introductory course as it dealt only with explaining how homing pigeons managed to find their way and how white mice succeeded in running through mazes. A different course in the second semester was better as it treated personality. In that course, taught by Professor Irving Child—I thought the name of the instructor was perfect for such a course—there was one week where the suggested reading was Otto Rank's *The Myth of the Birth of the Hero*. I should stress that the reading was optional, not required. Perhaps it was my early attraction to fairy tales that made me check out the book, but in any event, I can still recall the thrill of discovery as I read Rank's remarkable essay. Of course, I had no idea then that I would eventually try to follow in Rank's footsteps and that I would have the pleasure and honor of having my own essay "The Hero Pattern and the Life of Jesus" reprinted in the same volume with my idol's essay many years later (Rank, Raglan, and Dundes 1990). That book opened up the Freudian universe for me, and I then turned to Freud himself, which I read with equal delight. I was still unaware of the existence of the field of folkloristics, however.

It was the second turning point that was most crucial. Returning to Yale after two years active duty in the U.S. Navy Reserve, I was enrolled in the Master of Arts in the Teaching of English program, preparing to become a secondary school teacher. One of the courses I was taking was with Cleanth Brooks, one of the major forces in New Criticism. I had been unable to get into his classes as an undergraduate and felt privileged to have an opportunity to study with such an important literary critic. The course was devoted to "Modern Fiction Studies," in which we read Yeats and Faulkner, among other writers. One day, I mentioned to Professor Brooks that although I was very much enjoying the readings, especially Yeats, I wondered if I could study some of the Celtic mythology that Yeats drew upon for his poetry. His response was that such material was merely background for great literature and not really worthy of my consideration. Fortunately, I was also taking a course in the nineteenth-century English novel with Paul Pickrel. I asked Professor Pickrel more or less the same question. I told him I liked reading the Thomas Hardy novels but what I was especially intrigued by was Hardy's frequent allusions to rural customs and the like. And that was precisely the moment when my life took a huge unexpected turn. Professor Pickrel said, "There's a place you can go to study that sort of thing. It's Illinois or Indiana or one of those." I was sufficiently motivated by this suggestion that I went shortly thereafter to the section of the university library where course catalogs from other colleges were shelved. I started by looking at the University of Illinois catalog since Professor Pickrel had mentioned that university first. Under "English," I found the usual courses in Chaucer, Spenser, Shakespeare, and so forth. Nothing unusual there. Then I picked up the Indiana University catalog and looked under "English." Again, there were courses in Chaucer, Spenser, Shakespeare, and so forth, but then I saw a course in "The English and Scottish Traditional Ballad" and another in "The Folktale." Underneath those courses was a note saying "See also under 'Folklore.'" I turned the page from "English" to "Folklore," and was astonished to see that Indiana University had a department of folklore offering a doctorate in that subject. That was it. I knew then what I wanted to do with my life. After a year in France teaching conversational English at a boys' lycée in Colmar following my marriage to my long-suffering wife, Carolyn, we spent three years (1959–62) in Bloomington, Indiana, where I earned my Ph.D. in folklore.

So I was finally able to combine my earlier interest in Freud with my chosen field of study: folklore. However, I should probably also mention that despite having superb instructors at Indiana University, my plan to become a psychoanalytic folklorist was not encouraged. Quite the contrary, it was discouraged. I soon realized that I would not be able to write a psychoanalytically informed dissertation.

Two incidents occurred during my graduate years with respect to my psychoanalytic orientation, and I shall mention them because I believe they are emblematic of the extreme prejudice against psychoanalysis that sadly continues to prevail in the academy. One of my important mentors at Indiana was Professor Erminie Wheeler-Voegelin who I later learned was the daughter of Benjamin Ide Wheeler, one of the early presidents of the University of California, Berkeley, for whom Wheeler Hall on the Berkeley campus is named. She offered courses in North and South American Indian folklore, and I enrolled in both of them. In the first course, one of my fellow students, Elli Köngäs (later Köngäs-Maranda) from Finland gave a detailed oral report on the "Earth-Diver" myth. (The report was published in 1960 in the journal *Ethnohistory*.) Professor Wheeler-Voegelin was herself an authority on the myth, having written the entry on it for the *Standard Dictionary of Folklore, Mythology and Legend*. The plot involves a series of animals, usually four, the ritual number for most native American peoples, diving deep down into the primeval floodwaters seeking a particle of mud. The last animal, for example, a muskrat, succeeds in bringing up a tiny bit of mud, which expands magically to form the earth. A widespread myth, found in Asia, the Americas, and Eastern Europe, it has been much studied by folklorists. When I heard the oral report, I could see immediately that it was a classic case of male anal erotic creativity (in which males attempt to compete with females by creating from a substance produced by their bodies). I said as much in the seminar and was ridiculed by all assembled for this seemingly bizarre interpretation. I was sufficiently annoyed by this total rejection of my idea that I was inspired to write a paper on the subject that was later published in the *American Anthropologist* in 1962. I well remember Professor Wheeler-Voegelin's friendly prediction that I would surely "outgrow" my Freudian tendencies in time. So far I have not.

Professor Wheeler-Voegelin served on my dissertation committee, but my principal advisor was Professor Richard M. Dorson, the chair of the Folklore Program. We eventually became very close friends. But at one point during my first year at Indiana, Professor Dorson surprised me by saying he wanted to take me to lunch. This was unusual as professors did not do this as a rule. I was flattered, of course, and soon thereafter we had lunch at the Student Union cafeteria. After some polite conversation, he told me that he knew of my interest in psychoanalytic theory and that he had been commissioned to write a major article on folklore theories for *Current Anthropology* and wanted to include mention of the psychoanalytic approach. I was extremely pleased, first, that he was willing to write about the psychoanalytic approach to folklore and, second, that he thought enough of me to ask for my help in supplying references. I told him about my admiration for Otto Rank's *The Myth of the Birth of the Hero* and mentioned many other key sources. An initial brief essay was published in *Daedalus* in the spring of 1959, but the more complete version appeared in 1963, a year after I had left Indiana, and when I read it, I felt betrayed. Professor Dorson called "the psychoanalytical school that memorializes Sigmund Freud" the school of interpretation "most abhorrent to orthodox folklorists." He equated the psychoanalytic approach with solar mythology, implying that both were totally absurd. "Psychoanalytical readings of myths and folktales substitute sexual symbolism for the nineteenth-century symbolism of heavenly phenomena." Dorson did ably summarize all the sources I had so carefully given him, but only for the purpose of making fun of them. Instead of helping my cause, I had unwittingly aided and abetted the enemy. I had foolishly thought my professor had an open mind and that he sincerely wanted to learn something about the approach. Far from contributing to a greater understanding of the psychoanalytic approach to folklore, I had provided much of the ammunition used by Dorson to demean and ridicule it.

The attitudes of Professors Wheeler-Voegelin and Dorson were not in the least atypical. Archer Taylor, professor of German at the University of California, Berkeley, unquestionably one of the twentieth century's greatest folklore scholars, needed only one sentence to dismiss the approach: "The endeavors to solve the mystery of folk-tales by the even more puzzling mysteries of psychoanalysis can now be laid on the shelf to gather dust" (1940:17). This, in my opinion, is a fine example of "wishful thinking" on Taylor's part. He would have liked to have seen the psychoanalytic approach laid to rest permanently. Stith Thompson, the other great American folklorist of the twentieth century, held a similar view. In his classic book *The Folktale,* Thompson commented on one psychological reading of a folktale: "This may be the explanation for this story, and I should not wish to deprive anyone of the privilege of believing so. But even in the search for the ultimate origins of a folktale, there is no reason to be absurd" (1951:100). Thompson's position is: "When the folklorist has done his best to discover *all* the facts about the life history of the tale, there *may* be room for the psychologist" (1951:448, emphasis added.) Since all the facts about a folktale can probably never be known, there will thus never be room for the psychologist. Moreover, why should the folklorist need to call in a psychologist in the first place to analyze his (the folklorist's) subject matter? Why can't the folklorist analyze folklore psychologically by him or herself? Lest the unwary reader wrongly assume that these antipsychology prejudices are strictly echoes from the past, let me quote from Lauri Honko, the current doyen of Finnish folklorists, who was kind enough to review my 1997 book *Two Tales of Crow and Sparrow: A Freudian Folkloristic Essay on Caste and Untouchability* in the *FF Network* for November 2000. After saying that I was once "one of the most widely read folklorists in the world," Honko continues: "In recent years, however, his readership may have grown thinner, or more silent at least, because of his strong predilection for Freudian theorising to which relatively few folklorists subscribe. Such a strong theory seems difficult to integrate into other forms of folkloristic thinking" (2000:24). Honko does admit that he does not regard himself as an expert on psychoanalysis but apparently that poses no barrier to criticizing it or those who utilize it to analyze folklore.

It should now be perfectly obvious that psychoanalytic folkloristics is hardly mainstream. I acknowledge that freely. For most folklorists it is as though Freud never lived. The question is: Can psychoanalytic theory materially help us understand folkloristic data? If it cannot, then I would agree that it should logically be abandoned. But if it can, then perhaps younger students with more open minds might wish to consider exploring it as a means of providing access to the fantasy content of folklore. I want to make clear that I am not at all concerned with the medical or therapeutic aspects of psychoanalysis. Many of Freud's patients seem not to have been cured, or, if they were, it took years and years to accomplish. Freud did not fully appreciate women's psychology (nor did most others of his generation); Freud certainly had some peculiar ideas about the Lamarckian inheritance of phylogenetic ideas. None of these likely faults in Freud's thinking are relevant, in my opinion. What is relevant to folklore is the range of concepts such as "projection" and "family romance" (the Oedipus and Electra complexes).

It is my hope that the seven psychoanalytically informed essays contained in this volume will demonstrate forcefully that Freudian concepts do indeed illuminate folkloristic data. Moreover, they offer persuasive explanations of phenomena that literal-minded folklorists have hitherto been unable to fathom. Some of the questions I have sought to answer include: why should a deity be influenced or impressed by a supplicant's denying him or herself nourishment? In other words, what is the reason for the presumed efficacy of ritual fasting to summon a deity? Why is it that vampires are thought to need to suck the blood (or milk) from a family member in order to resuscitate themselves? Why does the principal male character in one of our oldest recorded folktales, the ancient Egyptian tale of two brothers, emasculate himself when ostensibly he knows that he is totally innocent of the false charge of his older brother's wife that he tried to seduce her? What is the reason for the extraordinary appeal of the Disney version of Hans Christian Andersen's literary legend "The Little Mermaid"? What is the significance, if any, of a widespread little girl's ritual that involves attempts to crowd into a bathroom (at school or at home) in the hope of seeing a bloody woman's face in the mirror? What is the underlying rationale for the seemingly bizarre and cruel traditions associated with male fraternity hazing rituals? And, finally, what is the possible meaning of a rough boys' game found in Greece and throughout the Indo-European world in which one or more boys "ride" the back or backs of their opponents?

What unites all these essays is the unapologetic application of psychoanalytic principles to folklore. I would like to think that some future students of folklore will experience something like the excitement I had years ago when I first read Otto Rank's *The Myth of the Birth of the Hero*. Psychologists used to call such an event the "Aha!" experience, the exclamation indicating the extreme pleasure produced by arriving at some kind of sudden personal insight. (The "technical" definition of the "Aha" experience is "The reaction accompanying the moment of insight in problem-solving situations" [Chaplin 1968:16].) The proof of the pudding in this instance is whether or not one or more of these essays succeeds in yielding genuine insight into the folklore data in question. If so, and admittedly that is for the reader to judge, then perhaps the promise of psychoanalytic folkloristics may yet be fulfilled.

References Cited

Aarne, Antti, and Stith Thompson. 1961. *The Types of the Folktale*. Helsinki: Academia Scientiarum Fennica.
Ackerman, Robert. 1991. *The Myth and Ritual School*. New York: Garland.
Ben-Amos, Dan. 1994. Bettelheim among the Folklorists. *Psychoanalytic Review* 81:509–35.
Chaplin, James P. 1968. *Dictionary of Psychology*. New York: Dell.
Cocchiara, Giuseppe. 1981. *The History of Folklore in Europe*. Philadelphia: ISHI.
Dorson, Richard M. 1959. Theories of Myth and the Folklorist. *Daedalus* 88:280–90.
———. 1963. Current Folklore Theories. *Current Anthropology* 4:93–112.
Dundes, Alan. 1962. Earth-Diver: Creation of the Mythopoeic Male. *American Anthropologist* 64:1032–50.

———. 1985. The Psychoanalytic Study of Folklore. *Annals of Scholarship* 3(3):1–42.
Dundes, Alan, ed. 1999. *International Folkloristics*. Lanham: Rowman & Littlefield.
Freud, Sigmund. 1953. *A General Introduction to Psychoanalysis*. New York: Permabooks.
Honko, Lauri, and B. A. Viveka Rai. 2000. On Caste and Untouchability—Without Love. *FF Network* No. 20:24–28.
Köngäs, Elli Kaija. 1960. The Earth-Diver (Th. A 812). *Ethnohistory* 7:151–80.
Legman, Gershon. 1968. *Rationale of the Dirty Joke*. New York: Grove Press.
———. 1975. *No Laughing Matter*. New York: Breaking Point.
Propp, Vladimir. 1968. *Morphology of the Folktale*. Austin: University of Texas Press.
———. 1984. *Theory and History of Folklore*. Minneapolis: University of Minnesota Press.
Rank, Otto, Lord Raglan, and Alan Dundes. 1990. *In Quest of the Hero*. Princeton: Princeton University Press.
Roberts, Warren E. 1994. *The Tale of "The Kind and the Unkind Girls."* Detroit: Wayne State University Press.
Róheim, Géza. 1953. *The Gates of the Dream*. New York: International Universities Press.
———. 1992. *Fire in the Dragon and Other Psychoanalytic Essays on Folklore*. Princeton: Princeton University Press.
Segal, Robert A. 1998. *The Myth and Ritual Theory*. Oxford: Blackwell.
Taylor, Archer. 1940. Some Trends and Problems in Studies of the Folk-Tale. *Studies in Philology* 37:1–25.
Thompson, Stith. 1951. *The Folktale*. New York: Dryden Press.
Wheeler-Voegelin, Erminie. 1949. Earth Diver. In *Standard Dictionary of Folklore, Mythology and Legend*. Edited by Maria Leach. 334. New York: Funk & Wagnalls.

ACKNOWLEDGMENTS

I would like to thank, first of all, my daughter, Professor Lauren Dundes, a member of the sociology department of Western Maryland College, who was the senior coauthor of two of the essays included in this volume. The inspiration for the essay on Disney's "The Little Mermaid" came from her daughter (my granddaughter) Madeline's invitation to her grandfather that he watch the video with her on more than one occasion. After repeated viewings, the sociologist and the folklorist began their joint analysis that culminated in the "The Trident and the Fork" essay. Some time later, my daughter suggested that we work together on an analysis of hazing practices on college campuses. That collaboration resulted in the "The Elephant Walk" paper. It was a joy to work with Lauren, and I am grateful to her for permitting me to include our two coauthored papers in this book.

I also thank the following publishers and societies for their kindness in allowing me to reprint some of the essays in this volume.

"The Psychoanalytic Study of Religious Custom and Belief: Ritual Fasting, Self-Mutilation, and the *Deus Otiosus*" was initially published as the lead article in *Southern Folklore* 55 (1998): 3–14, and is reprinted with the permission of the University Press of Kentucky.

"The Vampire as Bloodthirsty Revenant: A Psychoanalytic Post-Mortem" first appeared in Alan Dundes, ed., *The Vampire: A Casebook* (Madison: University of Wisconsin Press, 1998), 159–75, © 1998, and is reprinted with the permission of the University of Wisconsin Press.

"Projective Inversion in the Ancient Egyptian 'Tale of Two Brothers' " has been accepted for publication in the *Journal of American Folklore* and is reprinted with the permission of the American Folklore Society. The paper was awarded the 2001 Robert J. Stoller Foundation Essay Award for the best paper in an annual prize competition for essays on psychoanalytically informed research in the behavioral sciences, social sciences, or humanities.

"The Trident and the Fork: Disney's 'The Little Mermaid' as a Male Construction of an Electral Fantasy" was published in *Psychoanalytic Studies* 2 (2000): 117–30, and is reprinted by permission of that journal <http://www.tandf.co.uk>.

"Bloody Mary in the Mirror: A Ritual Reflection of Pre-Pubescent Anxiety" first appeared in *Western Folklore* 57 (1998): 119–35, © 1998, and is reprinted by permission of the California Folklore Society.

"The Greek Game of *Makria Yaidoura* [Long Donkey]: An Adolescent Articulation of a Mediterranean Model of Masculinity," was published in *Thiteia: Essays in Honour of Emeritus Professor Michael G. Miraklis* (Athens: University of Athens and University of Ioannina, 2002) and is reprinted by permission of the festschrift volume's editor, Minas Al. Alexiadis, Professor of Folklore at the University of Athens.

Bloody Mary in the Mirror

I

The Psychoanalytic Study of Religious Custom and Belief

RITUAL FASTING, SELF-MUTILATION, AND THE
DEUS OTIOSUS

One of the possible approaches to the study of religious custom and belief utilizes the principles of psychoanalysis. There is an abundant literature devoted to the psychoanalytic consideration of religion (cf. Saffady 1976; Wallace 1990). Benjamin Beit-Hallahmi's annotated bibliography on the subject, revised in 1996, contains more than 2000 entries and this useful survey refers only to English-language books and articles. Had materials in other languages, e.g., French and German, been surveyed, that number could easily have been trebled or quadrupled.

According to a critique by Joel Kovel, "Freud was oddly preoccupied with religion considering that he held the subject in enormous contempt as a kind of universal neurosis and impediment to the maturation of the human species" (1990:69). To be sure, Freud himself spoke of his "complete negative attitude to religion, in any form and however attenuated" in a letter to his lifelong friend, Swiss clergyman Oskar Pfister, dated 16 October 1927, a proleptic letter apologizing in advance for his about-to-appear *The Future of an Illusion* (Meng and Freud 1963:110). In an earlier letter to Pfister dated 9 October 1918, he made a similar self-assessment in wondering, "Why was it that none of the pious ever discovered psychoanalysis? Why did it have to wait for a *completely godless* Jew?" (Meng and Freud 1963:63, emphasis mine).

It is in *The Future of an Illusion*, first published in 1927, that Freud most fully articulated his conception of religion. For Freud, there is an infantile prototype of religion. "For once before one has been in such a state of helplessness: as a little child in one's relationship to one's parents" (1949:29). Man "makes the forces of nature not simply in the image of men with whom he can associate as his equals . . . but he gives them the characteristics of the father, makes them into gods . . . thereby following . . . an infantile prototype" (30). "Now when the child grows up and finds that he is destined to remain a child forever, and that he can never do without protection against unknown and mighty powers, he invests these with the traits of the father-figure" (42). The only serious error in Freud's formulation of infant:parent::adult:god is the male bias. As Antoine Vergote puts it: "The whole of Freud's psychoanalysis of religion is an attempt to clarify the idea of God as an imaginary enlargement of the father figure" (1990:82).

This is not to argue that Freud was totally wrong in emphasizing the paternal component of religion. It is easy enough to see the validity of the idea of a father projection in the religions of our own culture. We commonly speak of "God the Father"—as we do also of "Mary, Mother of God." Catholic priests are addressed as "Father" and the nominal head of the Catholic Church on earth is the "pope," a term cognate with papa or father. From a Freudian point of view, this is no accident or coincidence. Moreover, the paternal bias of many religions in the West is deeper than the above examples might suggest. We have only to recall the path-breaking discovery of F. Max Müller, the foremost Indologist of the nineteenth century (despite the fact that he never once set foot in India). In his own immodest words, "If I were asked what I consider the most important discovery which has been made during the nineteenth century with respect to the ancient history of mankind, I should answer in the following short line: Sanskrit DYAUSH-PITAR = Greek ΖΕΤΣ ΠΑΤΗΡ = Latin JUPITER" (1885:626; cf. 1899:537–38; and Bartoli 1928). Now Müller's point was clearly philological and comparative; it was not at all psychoanalytic. He was seeking to demonstrate the Indo-European identity of Sanskrit, Greek, and Latin through indisputable cognates, in this instance for God-Father. (The initial "Ju" in Jupiter is a rendering of Zeus or deus meaning "god" while the "piter" portion of Jupiter is "father" as in "pater.")

In any event, the paternal basis of overtly patriarchal religions is quite explicit and is obvious enough once it is pointed out. The literature on religion as projection is substantial (cf. Banks 1973), in particular on God as a father projection (cf. Beit-Hallahmi and Argyle 1975; Vergote and Tamayo 1980).

Freud's male bias is apparent in his quick dismissal of the nurturant mother figure. Although he admits that "the mother, who satisfies hunger, becomes the first love-object, and certainly also the first protection against all the undefined and threatening dangers of the outer world" (1949:41), he insists nevertheless upon describing god in strictly male terms, that is, in terms of the father. He argues "the mother is soon replaced by the stronger father, and this situation persists from now on over the whole of childhood" (41). But it is by no means clear that the mother is so inevitably displaced by the father. The existence of female deities, often stronger and more powerful than male deities, would argue against the Freudian male model. (Curiously, the evolutionary notion of initial early mother goddesses being replaced or displaced by later father gods would lend support to Freud's model.)

There was another theoretical problem with orthodox psychoanalytic theory which prevented it from being seriously considered by folklorists and others interested in religious custom and belief. That problem was the unwarranted assumption of pan-human universality. Beit-Hallahmi in his review of the psychoanalytic study of religion makes an unequivocal statement to this effect: "Psychoanalysis assumes the psychic unity of mankind, which is significant when we deal with cultural traditions. ... This assumed universality of psychoanalysis is definitely tied to a universalistic humanistic assumption of human brotherhood" (1996:5). Unless psychoanalytic theory could successfully accommodate the principles of cultural relativism developed and championed by anthropologists, among others, it remained highly unlikely that any reputable scholar would be tempted to employ psychoanalytic concepts in studying religion. The problem was in part solved by psychoanalyst Abram Kardiner who had been analyzed by Freud himself (Kardiner 1977). Thanks to the influence of anthropologist Ralph Linton with whom Kardiner taught a joint seminar at Columbia University in 1940—the joint seminar had begun in 1935 at the New York Psychoanalytic Institute (Linton and Wagley 1971:53–5)—Kardiner succeeded in culturally relativizing psychoanalytic theory. (For more on Kardiner, see Manson 1988.)

Kardiner's point of departure was Freud's position in *The Future of an*

6   Ritual Fasting, Self-Mutilation, and the *Deus Otiosus*

Illusion. In *The Individual and His Society*, published in 1939, Kardiner stated that although infants are by their very biological nature born helpless, they "do not perceive their helplessness, but on the contrary, feel as if they control the world" (35). This is because the parents or parent surrogates recognize the helplessness of the infant and consequently the necessary aid or assistance critical for survival is voluntarily given, e.g., the infant cries, a parent comes to its aid. From the infant's view, this results in feelings Freud called the "omnipotence of thought."[1] In other words, the infant feels hunger pangs, cries, and the parent or parent-surrogate provides nourishment or sustenance almost immediately. In Kardiner's terms, the infant soon learns that "he must do certain things with regard to the parent whose magical aid he wants to enlist" (1939:38). If religion truly is a projective system, a projective system modeled after the initial infantile perception of parent or parent-surrogate, then we can readily appreciate Kardiner's insight that "The technique used to solicit aid from the deity must in every way conform to the character of the discipline imposed on the child by the disciplinarians" (75). To this principle, we must now add the tenet of cultural relativism. Kardiner articulated this well in his sequel volume, *The Psychological Frontiers of Society*, published in 1945. He remarked that "In Tanala the relation of the individual to the ancestral gods seemed strikingly like the relation of the child to the parent in this culture" (23). But here is the important caveat. This particular relationship did not obtain in all cultures. "In other words, according as the [infantile] experience varied, so did the problem of the *projective systems* in folklore and religion" (23).

Therefore if we combine Freud's insight in *The Future of an Illusion* that infant is to parent as adult is to deity with Kardiner's necessary stipulation that infant-parent relationships vary from culture to culture, that is, the principle of cultural relativism, we can account for the diversity of adult-deity relationships cross-culturally. It is precisely the methodological possibility of culturally relativizing Freud's original model which makes it viable for folklorists and others to use it to study religious custom and belief.

I should like to illustrate the potential utility of psychoanalytic theory for this purpose with reference to three different topics: religious or ritual fasting, self-mutilation, and the so-called *deus otiosus*.

The first topic to be briefly considered is religious fasting. The intentional abstention from food "as a religious practice is a world-wide phenomenon" (Arbesmann 1949–1951:1) and can be observed in a number of world religions (cf. Gerlitz 1955). In a study by two Dutch scholars, we were reminded that "Fasting was regarded in various cultures as an obvious means of receiving dreams, visions and revelations of higher powers" and "Before consulting their oracles the ancient Greeks practised fasting as preparation for religious experiences or divine revelations, i.e., a meeting with God" (Wander Eycken and Van Deth 1994:16).

Another common function of ritual fasting occurs in the form of the so-called hunger strike. Hunger strikes as practiced by Gandhi in India to bring the colonialist British rulers to heel—Gandhi undertook seventeen fasts "to the death" (Erikson 1969:351)—or by prisoners to demand attention from their jailors may well be "an especially twentieth-century phenomenon" (Wander Eycken and Van Deth 1994:74), but the critical question is why should individuals think that by abstaining from nourishment they will force authorities in power to yield to their demands?

In the scholarship devoted to fasting, there is little agreement as to the origin or underlying rationale of the custom. J. A. MacCulloch in the *Hastings Encyclopaedia of Religion and Ethics* states, "Probably no single cause can be alleged as the origin of the practice of fasting" (1925:759). This sentiment is echoed by Rudolph Arbesmann in his erudite essay on fasting in pagan and Christian antiquity: "It cannot be traced back to one common motive" (1949–1951:1). Finnish anthropologist Edward Westermarck in his 1907 paper, "The Principles of Fasting," tends to favor the idea that fasting is a response to the threat of pollution (404), although it is by no means clear why food which on other occasions is perfectly acceptable and non-polluting should suddenly become irritating or offensive to a deity. Westermarck also notes that fasting may in some instances excite "compassion" from a deity (418), although he is forced to speculate that if fasting "implies suffering . . . the conclusion is drawn that the god delights in such suffering" (419). Karl Menninger in his brilliant 1938 treatise, *Man Against Himself,* asks essentially the same question: "Why the idea should have arisen that suffering is pleasing to God is difficult to understand unless one accepts the theory that it was supposed to appease and disarm an avenging power" (121). In 1996, in his full-length book on self-mutilation, psychiatrist Armando R. Favazza

8   Ritual Fasting, Self-Mutilation, and the *Deus Otiosus*

asks the question again: "Why are sacrifice and a focus on suffering so important to religion?" (29; cf. Bowker 1975).

The question is not just why should a god delight in the suffering of his devotee, but also why is fasting in particular carried out to please a deity? Menninger's view is "The tendency to starve oneself is more obscure in origin unless one dismisses the matter by saying that fasting is merely an effective way of suffering...." (121). Menninger goes on to say, "But for a more specific explanation of the tendency to deny the appetite for food, then, we must again go back to the childhood situation.... The little child may wish to secure attention, excite pity and concern, to exert power over his parents, or to defy or exasperate them by not eating" (122). I believe Menninger was on the right track here, but unfortunately he follows this insight with the suggestion that "deeper than all these motives" is the imagined danger connected with the act of eating which in turn is "connected with infantile fantasies of eating people" (122). I am not necessarily denying the possibility of the existence of infantile cannibalistic wishes (as in eating or biting the mother's breast), but I do wonder whether such fantasies have anything to do with ritual fasting. Psychiatrist Favazza repeats Menninger's reasoning: "Children can express willful anger toward their parents either by refusing to eat or by spitting out their food" and that "This behavior may be the prototype of self-mutilation as a retaliation against an abusive adult" (1996:51). Again, this may be a valid insight, but it would not appear to explain the rationale underlying ritual fasting in a religious context.

Let us see if ethnographic data can illuminate the issue. Jules Blumensohn in his 1933 survey of "The Fast Among North American Indians" claims that the Central Algonkian used the fast to establish *"a personal relation* with the supernatural" (451) and specifically used fasting to "arouse the commiseration" or pity of the supernatural beings (455). He quotes one of Paul Radin's Winnebago informants who told a tale in which the protagonist "So that he might be blessed by the spirits ... starved and thirsted himself to death; he made himself pitiable in their sight" (466) and the spirits responded.

Another Winnebago account confirms the technique but adds some crucial details. A Yale-educated Winnebago, Henry Roe Cloud, born in 1884, made the following revealing statement: "Fasting is a universal practice among Indians. Sometimes they go without food from four to ten days at a time. The purpose of these fasts, in which I often took part, is to gain the compassion and blessing of some spirit, *in order that he may come and reveal himself*" (Dundes 1963:214, emphasis mine).

There is more than a hint in Cloud's personal statement that the act of fasting compels the spirit to "come and reveal himself." This element of compulsion is critical. James George Frazer, citing Franz Boas, remarks that the Tsimshian "think they can compel the deity to grant their wishes by observing a rigid fast" (1910:317; cf. Arbesmann 1949–1951:22). From these comments, we can see that the early theorists were totally wrong in thinking that fasting "pleased" the supernatural spirits. Rather, fasting is a means of exerting power because it "forces" these spirits to approach the supplicant. By what logic or "psycho" logic can it be deemed reasonable to assume that fasting can force a deity or guardian spirit or other supernatural being to approach? From a psychoanalytic perspective, it is perfectly obvious. If an infant associates feeling hunger pangs with the coming of an adult parent or parent-surrogate, then the adult who wants a deity to approach must clearly make himself hungry. Moreover, the hungrier he is, the more likely it is that the parent-deity will approach.

Now we are in a position to better appreciate some of the previous theorizing about fasting. W. Robertson-Smith in his classic *Lectures on the Religion of the Semites* suggested that there "are very strong reasons for believing that . . . fasting is primarily nothing more than a preparation for the sacramental eating of holy flesh" (1894:434). The holy flesh would presumably be wholly flesh, that is, the original maternal breast. Eileen Farrell in her insightful essay, "The Poetics of Renunciation: Form and Content in Ritual Fasting," explains the Ramadhan fast in such terms when she maintains that "ritual fasting transforms enforced deprivation into joyous feasting" and thus "evokes the most primitive wish-fulfillment of all, the moment when the hungry infant regains its mother's breast" (1985:254). With this infantile logic, it makes perfect sense for hunger artists like Gandhi to think that abstinence from food will force the government authorities to come to him and grant his wishes. Through the "omnipotence of thought," the adult thinks that fasting compels the authority figure to come to his aid. Analogous logic might also explain the strange fasting custom whereby a creditor fasts on a debtor's doorstep to force him to pay up (Robinson 1909). This theory can also help clarify the *absence* of ritual fasting. In our own American culture when infants are either fed on demand or on a prescribed rigid schedule, we can understand why ritual fasting might not be perceived as an efficacious means of soliciting aid from a deity. Since the infant is not permitted to feel strong pangs of hunger—the parent comes automatically on schedule or at the first cry—the adult in such a society does not engage in extensive fasting. Instead an older fasting tradition may be supplanted by a simplified symbolic gesture. One food may be given up or the fasting lasts for just one day. Fasting practices would thus tend to change as infantile feeding practices change.

Let us now turn to our second topic: self-mutilation in a religious context. Self-mutilation covers a wide variety of body injuries ranging from wrist cuts, cigarette burns, and other such self-inflicted physical harm to more drastic acts such as self-flagellation and even auto-castration (Walsh and Rosen 1988:4). In psychiatric parlance, it is sometimes referred to as "The Deliberate Self-Harm Syndrome" (Pattison and Kahan 1983). Self-mutilation, especially as a religious ritual or custom, has long proved an enigma. Psychiatrist Favazza, who has devoted an entire book to the subject of self-mutilation, the second edition of which was published in 1996, confesses, "The more I examined self-mutilation, the more puzzling it seemed" (xii). Favazza is, however, more concerned with the "self-mutilation of the mentally ill" rather than "sacred" mutilations sanctioned by a particular community. He offers the following suggestion: "Self-mutilative ritual sacrifice and atonement are especially pleasing to spirits . . ." (227), a notion which is reminiscent of explanations offered with respect to ritual fasting, as noted above. The key question is why should spirits be "pleased" by self-mutilation by a supplicant? Karl Menninger, in his pioneering effort in 1935 to categorize self-mutilation, lists "religious self-mutilations" as the second of his six categories (422–33, repr. as 1938:248–61). The range of religious self-mutilation is extensive. Examples run the gamut from piercing one's tongue with a skewer among the Tamils, (cf. Collins 1997:4) to self-flagellation with whips or chains.

To answer the question of why a deity should be presumed to be influenced or impressed in any way by a devotee's infliction of bodily pain upon him or herself, we may first consider some of the research relevant to this behavior. One comprehensive investigation of self-mutilation suggests that the intent of the self-mutilator is to make a demand of some kind, either to "restore a terminated relationship or to gain dominance in an interpersonal conflict" (Walsh and Rosen 1988:88). Another study proposes that the most popular explanation of self-injurious behavior is that it "is a form of reinforced attention seeking.... It gives the child a means of controlling the behavior of those around him" (deCatanzaro 1978:47). Favazza, after mentioning *en passant* that suicide attempts have been called "a cry for help," comments, "Sometimes self-mutilation can be a manipulative ploy to gain attention or to coerce others into providing a caring, mothering response" (1996:276–77). Common, apparently is the idea that the mutilator threatens to indulge in self-harmful behavior unless his or her demands are met. Typically a parent is so threatened. All of the comments cited above, however, refer to self-mutilation in general, not to religious customs.

If we again recall the equation, child is to parent as adult is to deity, then I believe we can better understand religious customs involving self-mutilation. In fact, the answer to the question of why the self-infliction of body pain by an individual should be considered a reasonable technique to gain the attention of a deity and to "coerce" that deity into noticing the supplicant is absurdly simple. If we remember that human actions aimed at the supernatural, at a deity, can be construed as projections of infantile behavior towards parents or parent-surrogates, then it is surely obvious that one foolproof method of attracting a parent is to cry out in pain, preferably with actual blood showing. Just as a parent is virtually forced to deal with an infant or small child who is hurt, e.g., bleeding, so a deity has no choice other than to direct his or her attention to a supplicant-adult in apparent or real pain. The fact that the pain is self-induced is not relevant insofar as a parent, despite being annoyed at the seemingly unnecessary plight of the infant-child, has no alterative but to attend to the infant-child in distress. An infant who is hurt "coerces" the parent or parent-surrogate to approach. Indeed, it may be the only viable technique available in the case of an apathetic or indifferent parent. With this psychoanalytic insight, the various forms of religious self-mutilation make sense. Though typically adjudged to be bizarre behavior, these forms represent a perfectly logical thought process, albeit unconscious, manifested in a series of actions designed to attract the favorable notice of a deity which in effect compel him or her to pay attention to the supplicant. Without psychoanalytic theory, these seemingly excessive masochistic practices must remain aberrant behavior apparently totally irrational in nature.

The third and last example of the application of psychoanalytic theory to religious custom and belief is the so-called *deus otiosus*. The term refers to a creator god, frequently male, who withdraws after the initial act of creation and functions thereafter as a remote and distant figure, virtually immune from direct contact with men on earth. Other terms for the *deus otiosus* include *deus remotus* and *deus abscondidus* (Nwanunobi 1984:147). The enigmatic figure of *deus otiosus* has been a subject of a running debate about its possible significance, which continued through the second half of the twentieth century (O'Connell 1962; Horton 1962; James 1962; Long 1963; Shelton 1964, 1965; Shack 1980; Nwanunobi 1984). Two of the intellectual giants in the study of comparative religion, Raffaele Pettazzoni and Mircea Eliade, were both intrigued by the issue. Pettazzoni wondered, "How can we explain this *otiositas* which contrasts so strikingly with the highly dynamic character of the Creator?" His answer is that ". . . *otiositas* itself belongs to the essential nature of creative beings" insofar as it pushes him into the background. "The world once made and the cosmos established, the Creator's work is as good as done" (1954:32). Eliade in his discussion of *deus otiosus* in *Patterns in Comparative Religion* (1974:46–59) cites an apt Bantu summary of the phenomenon: "God, after having made man, pays no further attention to him" (49). The bulk of the discussion has tended to center on West Africa, a typical locus being Nigeria. Victor C. Uchendu, for example, in his study of the Igbo, remarks, "The Igbo high god is a withdrawn god. He is a god who has finished all active works of creation and keeps watch over his creatures from a distance" (1965:94).

An African scholar, Onyeka Nwanunobi, criticizes Western writers on the subject, accusing them of speculating about the meaning of *deus otiosus* without sufficient attention to ethnographic data from the cultures in question. Their overly intellectual concern with the concept of "high gods" or "supreme deities" has, in his view, wrongly influenced their interpretation of the subject. Nwanunobi contends instead that "The interpretation of otiositas should rather be sought in [the] prevalent form of interpersonal relationship in the societies in which this phenomenon obtains" (1984:152). He suggests that in traditional Igbo society transactional communications are always characterized by the utilization of intermediaries such as brokers or middlemen. Accordingly, the supreme creator must be distant so as to allow a comparable role for so-called "minor spirits" to carry messages to and from the supreme being.

Nwanunobi is on the right track. but he might have profited from utilizing the Kardinerian revision of the Freudian paradigm to explain the *deus otiosus* more fully. The key theoretical concept, one should keep in mind, is that theology and mythology constitute an authentic and accurate ethnographic projection of parent-child relationships in a given culture, as Philip Slater so brilliantly demonstrates in *The Glory of Hera* (1968). From this perspective, the absence of the supreme (male) creator could be correlated with another critical factor common in African social organization, namely, the practice of polygamous marriages and the consequent existence of co-wives with separate huts for such wives. Each household thus consists of a mother and her children. The father moves from one household to another in some kind of rotation. In other words, he creates (procreates) and then departs. From the infant's perspective, the father does not appear to be a permanent member of the household in the same sense that the mother is. In that infantile context, it makes perfect sense for the religious projective system to include a male creator who withdraws after the act of creation and who remains a distant figure to be approached only through mediators or brokers. It would also explain why the *deus otiosus* is not found very often in the West with its monogamous marriage system and basic nuclear family household. Although there may be absent-father households in the West, the temporarily absent father may eventually return home to his single-family permanent residence.

One last point about the Kardinerian revision of the Freudian model: It is in the final analysis empirically testable. Whether the hypothetical explanations for the custom of ritual fasting, religious self-mutilation, and the *deus otiosus* here proposed are valid or not, they can surely be investigated. Either there is a parallelism or isomorphism or congruence between infantile conditioning in a culture and that culture's projective systems, or there is not. One does not have to accept these hypothetical explanations on faith. Testing psychoanalytic hypotheses in the field or against empirical ethnographic data is absolutely critical if the psychoanalytic approach to folklore is ever to gain credence or credibility among mainstream folklorists and others concerned with religious custom and belief.

Note

1. This memorable phrase, by the way, Freud learned from one of his patients, an educated lawyer, the so-called Rat Man (Jones 1955:266 n.g), just as folklorists and anthropologists gain many of their most treasured insights from key informants.

References Cited

Arbesmann, Rudolph, 1949–1951. Fasting and Prophecy in Pagan and Christian Antiquity. *Tradition* 7:1–71.
Banks, Robert. 1973. Religion as Projection: A Re-Appraisal of Freud's Theory. *Religious Studies* 9:401–26.
Bartoli, Matteo. 1928. La Monogenesi di Theos e Deus. *Revista di filologia e di istruzione classica* 56:108–17.
Beit-Hallahmi, Benjamin. 1996. *Psychoanalytic Studies of Religion: A Critical Assessment and Annotated Bibliography*. Westport, Connecticut: Greenwood Press.
Beit-Hallahmi, Benjamin and Michael Argyle. 1975. God as a Father-Projection: The Theory and the Evidence. *British Journal of Medical Psychology* 48:71–5.
Blumensohn, Jules, 1933. The Fast Among North American Indians. *American Anthropologist* 35:451–69.
Bowker, John. 1975. *Problems of Suffering in Religions of the World*. Cambridge, Massachusetts: Cambridge University Press.
Collins, Elizabeth Fuller. 1997. *Pierced By Murugan's Lance. Ritual, Power, and Moral Redemption among Malaysian Hindus*. DeKalb, Illinois: Northern Illinois University Press.
deCatanzaro, Denys A. 1978. Self-Injurious Behavior: A Biological Analysis. *Motivation and Emotion* 2:45–65.
Dundes, Alan. 1963. Summoning Deity Through Ritual Fasting. *American Imago* 20:213–20.
Eliade, Mircea. 1974. *Patterns in Comparative Religion*. New York: New American Library.
Erikson, Erik H. 1969. *Gandhi's Truth*. New York: W.W. Norton.
Farrell, Eileen. 1985. The Poetics and Renunciation: Form and Content in Ritual Fasting. *Journal of Psychoanalytic Anthropology* 8:249–64.
Favazza, Armando R. [1987] 1996. *Bodies Under Siege: Self-Mutilation and Body Modification in Culture and Psychiatry*. 2nd ed. Baltimore: The Johns Hopkins University Press.
Frazer, James George. 1910. *Totemism and Exogamy*. Vol. III. London: Macmillan.
Freud, Sigmund. 1949. *The Future of an Illusion*. London: The Hogarth Press.
Gerlitz, Peter. 1955. Das Fasten im Religionsgeschichtlichen Vergleich. *Zeitschrift für Religions- und Geistegeschichte* 7:116–26.
Horton, Robin. 1962. The High God: A Comment on Father O'Connell's Paper. *Man* 62:137–40.
James. E. O. 1962. The Withdrawal of the High God in West African Religion. *Man* 62:106.
Jones, Ernest. 1955. *The Life and Work of Sigmund Freud*. Vol. 2. New York: Basic Books.
Kardiner, Abram. 1939. *The Individual and His Society*. New York: Columbia University Press.
———. 1945. *The Psychological Frontiers of Society*. New York: Columbia University Press.
———. 1977. *My Analysis with Freud: Reminiscences*. New York: W.W. Norton.
Kovel, Joel. 1990. Beyond the Future of an Illusion: Further Reflections on Freud and Religion. *Psychoanalytic Review* 77:69–86.
Linton, Adelin, Charles Wagley. 1971. *Ralph Linton*. New York: Columbia University Press.
Long, Charles H. 1963. The West African High God: History and Religious Experience. *History of Religions* 3:328–42.

MacCulloch, J. A. 1925. Fasting. In *Hastings Encyclopaedia of Religion and Ethics*. Vol. V., 759–65. New York: Charles Scribner's Sons.
Manson, William C. 1988. *The Psychodynamics of Culture: Abram Kardiner and Neo-Freudian Anthropology*. Westport: Greenwood Press.
Meng. Heinrich and Ernst L. Freud, eds. 1963. *Psychoanalysis and Faith: The Letters of Sigmund Freud & Oskar Pfister*. New York: Basic Books.
Menninger, Karl A. 1935. A Psychoanalytic Study of the Significance of Self-Mutilations. *Psychoanalytic Quarterly* 4:408–66.
———. 1938. *Man Against Himself*. New York: Harcourt, Brace and Company.
Müller, F. Max. 1885. The Lesson of "Jupiter." *The Nineteenth Century* 18:626–50.
———. 1899. *The Science of Language*. Vol. II. London: Longmans, Green, and Co.
Nwanunobi. C. Onyeka. 1984. The Deus Otiosus Concept in Traditional Igbo Religion: An Examination through Transactional Analysis. *Anthropos* 79:145–54.
O'Connell, James. 1962. The Withdrawal of the High God in West African Religion: An Essay in Interpretation. *Man* 62:67–9.
Pattison, E. Mansell, and Joel Kahan. 1983. The Deliberate Self-Harm Syndrome. *American Journal of Psychiatry* 140:857–72.
Pettazzoni, Raffaele. 1954. *Essays on the History of Religions*. Leiden: E.J. Brill.
Robertson-Smith, W. [1889] 1894. *Lectures on the Religion of the Semites*. New Edition. London: Adam and Charles Black.
Robinson, F. N. 1909. Notes on the Irish Practice of Fasting as a Means of Distraint. In *Putnam Anniversary Volume: Anthropological Essays presented to Frederic Ward Putnam*, 567–83. New York: G.E. Stechert.
Saffady, William. 1976. New Developments in the Psychoanalytic Study of Religion: A Bibliographic Review of the Literature Since 1960. *Psychoanalytic Review* 63:291–99.
Shack, William A. 1980. On *Deus Otiosus* in Gurage Religious Traditions After the Accession of Menelik II. In *Modern Ethiopia*, ed. Joseph Tubiana, 491–99. Rotterdam: A.A. Balkema.
Shelton, Austin J. 1964. On Recent Interpretations of *Deus Otiosus:* The Withdrawn God in West African Psychology. *Man* 64:53–4.
———. 1965. The Presence of the "Withdrawn" High God in North Ibo Religious Belief and Worship. *Man* 65:15–9.
Slater, Philip E. 1968. *The Glory of Hera: Greek Mythology and the Greek Family*. Boston: Beacon Press.
Uchendu, Victor C. 1965. *The Igbo of Southeast Nigeria*. New York: Holt, Rinehart and Winston.
Vergote, Antoine. 1990. Confrontation with Neutrality in Theory and Praxis. In *Psychoanalysis and Religion*, ed. Joseph H. Smith and Susan A. Handelman, 79–94. Baltimore: The Johns Hopkins University Press.
Vergote, Antoine and Alvara Tamayo, eds. 1980. *The Parental Figures and the Representation of God: A Psychological and Cross-Cultural Study*. The Hauge: Mouton.
Wallace, Edwin R. 1990. Psychiatry and Religion: Toward a Dialogue and Public Philosophy. In *Psychoanalysis and Religion*, ed. Joseph H. Smith and Susan A. Handelman, 195–221. Baltimore: The John Hopkins University Press.
Walsh, Barent W., and Paul M. Rosen. 1988. *Self-Mutilation: Theory, Research, and Treatment*. New York: The Guilford Press.
Wander Eycken. Walter and Ron Van Deth. 1994. *From Fasting Saints to Anorexic Girls: The History of Self-Starvation*. New York: New York University Press.
Westermarck, Edward. 1907. The Principles of Fasting. *Folklore* 18:391–422.

2

The Vampire as Bloodthirsty Revenant

A PSYCHOANALYTIC POST MORTEM

In accordance with a pronounced penchant for the ritual number three, Western folklorists are prone to divide cultural materials into a tripartite classificatory scheme: elite culture, mass or popular culture, and folklore. Sometimes these admittedly somewhat arbitrary categories are mutually exclusive. That is, there are surely literary creations which have no analogs or parallels in either popular culture or folklore. By the same token there may be instances of popular culture (e.g., comic books, television programs, motion pictures, and the like) which are totally independent of both elite or high culture and folklore. In the same way, there may be folklore which is orally transmitted from person to person, from generation to generation, which has never served as the inspiration for either popular or elite culture.

Elite culture and popular culture, however, are more similar to one another than either is to folklore. Indeed, sometimes the line of demarcation between high culture and popular culture is very subjective. What makes a particular example from a popular-culture genre, such as a detective story, a tale of science fiction, a cowboy/outlaw Western adventure, or a silhouette romance, qualify as so-called high culture? In any event, both high and popular cultures are fixed in print or locked into videotape or film. In marked contrast, there are *always* multiple versions of folklore, versions which exhibit variation from one to another. A literary novel or a television program cannot change over time. They are necessarily the same for each new generation. True, the perception or reception of them can vary with succeeding sequences of audiences, but the texts themselves cannot change. Folklore, on the other hand, is constantly in a state of flux. No two versions of an item of folklore will be verbatim identical. Multiple existence (in more than one time and/or place) and variation are the hallmark criteria of folklore or oral tradition. In the majority of cases, there is another important distinguishing characteristic, namely, authorship. In most instances, the author of a literary work is known and so also are the authors of works in popular culture. We know who the creators of *Star Trek* and *Tarzan* are. The creators of folklore, however, are almost always anonymous.

The vampire (Motif E 251. Vampire. Corpse which comes from grave at night and sucks blood) is an example of a subject or topic which is found in all three levels of culture. There are literary treatments of the vampire in countless novels (and some *with* counts!), short stories and poems (see Marigny 1985; Carter 1989; Frost 1989); and there are depictions of the vampire in popular culture, for example, television ("Dark Shadows") and innumerable films (see Riccardo 1983; Melton 1994:719–774); and there are plenty of documentations of the vampire figure in folklore. Whereas we know who the authors of the literary renderings of the vampire are and whereas films involving vampires provide credits indicating who the writers of the screen play are, in contrast, we have absolutely no idea who the individual or individuals might have been who created the initial folkloristic figure of the vampire. We do not even know for certain where in the world the vampire first appeared. One thing we do know, however, is that the original source of both literary and popular cultural representations of the vampire came from folklore, not the other way round. Bram Stoker's *Dracula* of 1897 may well have influenced the literary works and films which appeared after that date, but Bram Stoker, an Irishman by birth, did not invent the Transylvanian vampire. That figure existed long before Stoker wrote his famous novel (see Florescu 1985–86; and Ryan 1993).

Because the vast bulk of vampire scholarship has tended to concentrate upon literary and popular cultural renderings of this curious and enigmatic creature, by design I shall limit my consideration of this figure to the folklore of the vampire. Actually, the vampire has attracted the attention of many folklorists of the past. Jacob Grimm in a posthumously published note to his *Deutsche Mythologie* defined vampires as "dead men come back, who suck blood" (Grimm 1966:1586). Other nineteenth-century folklorists writing about vampires include Mannhardt (1859), Hanush (1859), Krauss (1892a, 1982b), and Afanas'ev (1976). Twentieth-century folkloristic discussions have been penned by Polívka (1901), Vukanović (1957–59), Burkhart (1966), Oinas (1978, 1982), and Perkowsky (1976, 1989, 1992a, 1992b). There are also substantial surveys of vampire beliefs and legends in individual countries, for example, Bulgaria (Popov 1983; Beynen 1988), Czechoslovakia (Wollman 1920–23), Greece (du Boulay 1982), Romania (Weslowski 1910; Murgoci 1926; Nixon 1979; Cremene 1981; Perkowski 1982; Senn 1982), Russia (Jaworskij 1898; Afanas'ev 1976), and Serbia (Durham 1923; Djordjevic 1953). In Poland, a vampire questionnaire was issued, suggesting that belief in vampires persisted in that country into the twentieth century (Fischer 1927).

Widespread as the vampire is throughout eastern Europe, it is not true, as has been claimed, that "belief in vampires is found all over the world" (Anon. 1950:1154). This statement in the *Standard Dictionary of Folklore, Mythology and Legend* is demonstrably false. The vampire is *not* universal by any means. Native Americans do not have vampires. Nor do most of the indigenous peoples of Oceania have vampires. Fear of the dead is one thing; vampires in particular are quite another. (For that matter, there is not one single myth, legend, or folktale which is universal in the sense of being known by *all* human populations, past and present, as even the most cursory inspection of the six-volume *Motif-Index of Folk-Literature* clearly attests.) According to the encyclopedic *Vampire Book* (1994), a vampire "is a reanimated corpse that rises from the grave to suck the blood of living people and thus retain a semblance of life" or "a peculiar kind of revenant, a dead person who had returned to life and continued a form of existence through drinking the blood of the living" (Melton 1994:xxii, 629). Vampire discussions frequently include apotropaic measures to ward off vampire attacks (see Krauss 1892b; Jellinek 1904:323) as well as descriptions of time-tested techniques effective in killing them once and for all, for example, by driving a stake through their hearts or their navels (Murgoci 1926:328) or by decapitation (Wollman 1923:143).

In reviewing what is known about the vampire, we may mention the term itself. What is the meaning or significance, if any, of the word *vam-*

pire? One theory proposes a Turkish origin for the term (Naylor 1983:95; Wilson 1985:577), but there seems to be consensus that the source of the word is the Slavic *vampir* (Bielfeldt 1971; Naylor 1983; Wilson 1985; Perkowski 1989:32–33). As for the possible semantic significance of *vampire*, one theory, supported by the great nineteenth-century Russian folklorist A. N. Afanas'ev, suggests that the term derives from the Greek root $p\bar{\imath}$, meaning "to drink" (Afanas'ev 1976:164; see also Marigny 1986:168 and Buck 1949:331). Although one modern researcher finds this theory "attractive," he refers to problems with it (Naylor 1983:97). I shall argue later that this theory is extremely plausible.

The attempts to interpret the basic meaning of the vampire figure may for the sake of convenience be divided into two broad categories: literal-historical and metaphoric-symbolic. The literal-historical approach is exemplified by the prolific writings of Montague Summers, who seems to have believed that there are in fact actual vampires. In his words, "For the hauntings of a Vampire, three things are necessary: the Vampire, the Devil, and the Permission of Almighty God." Summers is not sure whether it is the Devil who energizes the corpse or whether the deceased reappears by himself through "some dispensation of Divine Providence." Each case must be decided individually on its own merits. Can the Devil really do this? Summers' unequivocal answer: "There is no doubt the Demon can do this" (1995:174). A host of parapsychological essays on the vampire argue in a similar vein (Riccardo 1983:91–99). Yet another instance of the "literal" approach is represented by those psychologists who contend that the vampire legend is based upon clinical cases of mentally disturbed individuals who drink the blood of their victims (see Vanden Bergh and Kelly 1964; Prins 1984, 1985; Jaffé and DiCataldo 1994; and Bourguignon 1997). A more reasoned illustration of the literal-historical approach is Paul Barber's 1988 *Vampires, Burial, and Death*, in which he seeks to demonstrate that all the alleged physical characteristics of the vampire correspond to the physiological reality of corpses in the process of decomposition. For Barber, folklore consists of history encumbered by a legendary overlay, and the task he sets himself is to deconstruct that overlay to find the kernel of historical truth contained therein (1987:3; 1988:152). It is the folk's empirical observation of corpses, he contends, that has led to the creation of the vampire imago. For example, since the tongue of a corpse may protrude and since blood may seep from its open mouth, observers wrongly assumed that the vampire must attack his victims "with teeth or tongue and suck their blood" (1988:157, 195–196). Barber's sophisticated reliance on forensic pathology makes his discussion plausible, but it falls well short of offering a satisfactory explanation of what is almost certainly fantasy, not reality.

Before discussing a possible metaphoric-symbolic interpretation of the vampire, I should like to mention two specific characteristics of the vampire which I believe any persuasive theory of the vampire must account for. Because descriptions of the vampire in various cultures abound, I shall not review all aspects of the creature here (see Summers, 1995, 1996; Melton 1994).

The first characteristic is the vampire's invariable return to attack "those who on earth have been his nearest and dearest" (Nixon 1979:18; see also Scierup 1986:179). There is even a Greek idiom, "The vampire hunts its own kindred" (du Boulay 1982:232) or, in an earlier rendering, the vampire "feeds on his own" (Bent 1886:397), which supports the notion that the vampire is connected somehow with family dynamics. Twitchell, in his essay "The Vampire Myth" (the reader is reminded that narratives about vampires are *legends,* stories told as true and set in postcreation time, *not myths,* which are sacred narratives explaining how the world and humankind came into being), even goes so far as to comment, "The most startling part of the folkloric vampire is that he must first attack members of his own family" (1980:86).

The second curious characteristic requiring an explanation is the belief that the vampire sometimes drinks milk rather than blood. Ernest Jones in his pioneering essay on the vampire notes this feature when he comments: "The German Alp sucks the nipples of men and children, and withdraws milk from women and cows more often than blood. The Drud also sucks the breasts of children, while the Southern Slav Mora sucks blood or milk indifferently" (1971:119). In Romania, we are told that vampires on St. George's Eve "take milk away from nursing mothers" (Murgoci 1926:332).

These two features of vampires—the attempt to attack close family members and the reported efforts of the vampire to drink milk rather than blood—are at first glance somewhat puzzling. But surely the most perplexing question to be explained is, Why do vampires need to suck the blood (or milk) of the living to facilitate a kind of life after death? Why, in sum, is the vampire a "bloodthirsty revenant"?

To answer this fundamental question, we need to place the vampire phenomenon in a wider theoretical framework. That structural framework, apparently common to Indo-European and Semitic worldview in antiquity, involves a set of bisecting humoral binary oppositions: hot and cold, and wet and dry. To this very day, folk disease theory depends upon combinations of these distinctions; for example, diseases (and cures) are classified as being "hot" or "cold." The word *sick* in English—about which, by the way, the OED claims, "Relationship to other Teutonic roots is uncertain, and no outside cognates have been traced"—is very likely a derivative of the Latin *siccus*, meaning "dry" (cf. *sec* in French). In classical Greek thought, we are told that "the Greeks conceived the living as 'wet' and the dead as 'dry' " (Lloyd 1964:101). Perhaps the best articulation of the principle that liquid is life and drying is dying was made by Richard Broxton Onians in his brilliant tour de force entitled *The Origins of European Thought about the Body, the Mind, the Soul, the World, Time, and Fate*, first published in 1951. According to Onians, life is perceived as a process whereby liquid gradually diminishes until the final desiccation, which is death (1973:214–215). I myself have earlier observed that it is possible to argue by analogy. Indo-European peoples could easily see the evolution, or more aptly the devolution, of grapes into raisins, plums into prunes, and so on, with this *se*cular transition marked by the appearance of wrinkles. So as older men and women became wrinkled with the onset of advancing age, these wrinkles could perfectly logically be interpreted as the consequences of a drying-out process (Dundes 1980:102–103). In this context we can understand why the replenishment of liquid lost, as a means of rejuvenation, is such a common theme, with manifestations as varied as the search for the fountain of youth and the application of ointments and oils to aging skin.

Closer to the vampire issue, we can also appreciate the specifics of various death and burial practices. In modern Greece, we find the custom of "breaking vessels filled with water on the tombs of departed friends" (Onians 1973:272; see also Sartori 1908). Politis, the founder of Greek folkloristics, in an essay on this custom, comments that "the water held by these broken vessels was an offering to the dead" and that "it refreshes the departed" (1894:35, 41). He reports further, "In Crete a jar full of water is deposited at the grave, where it is left for forty days, the belief being that during all that time the departed soul wanders over the haunts where it lived, and returns every evening to drink of the water provided" (1894:37). Some have argued that the broken vessel is a symbol of the deceased and that "the pouring out of the water symbolizes the vanishing soul and the dead body will fall to pieces like the broken crock. Others say that they pour out the water "in order to allay the burning thirst of the dead man" (Onians 1973:275). The antiquity of this ritual is confirmed by the Babylonian custom whereby the nearest kinsman of the deceased was obliged to serve as "pourer of water" at the grave or tomb. Hence a Babylonian curse: "May God deprive him of an heir and a pourer of water" (Onians 1973:285).

All this helps explain why the dead are perceived as being thirsty. Ever since Bellucci's 1909 essay, "Sul bisogno di dissetarsi attribuito all'anima dei morti," and Deonna's equally excellent 1939 discussion, "La soif des morts," this folkloristic conception of the thirsty dead has been amply documented. (There is also Sartori's 1908 cross-cultural survey, "Das Wasser in Totengebrauche.") So the vampire as a thirsty dead corpse fits very well into the standard Indo-European and Semitic worldview paradigm.

From this, we can now understand why the dead are so anxious to obtain liquid refreshment to become re-fleshed. But why the sucking act (which in the literary forms of the vampire was metamorphosed into biting)? To answer this question (as well as the associated question of why the very conception of life should be tied to liquid), we must have recourse to psychology.

The majority of psychological analyses of the vampire have concentrated almost exclusively on literary versions of this creature, with special emphasis on Bram Stoker's 1897 novel *Dracula*. (For useful reviews of this massive literature, see Margaret L. Shanahan's extensive entry, "Psychological Perspectives on Vampire Mythology," in *The Vampire Book* [in Melton 1994: 492–501], and the section "Psychoanalytical Approaches" in Leatherdale's *Dracula: The Novel & the Legend* [1985:160–175] and Gelder 1994.) There are also several clinical studies of patients exhibiting what is adjudged to be vampirelike behavior (see Yvonneau 1990; and Gottlieb 1991, 1994). Psychological or psychoanalytic studies of the folkloristic vampire proper are many fewer in number. Let us begin with Freud.

One of the sources cited by Freud in his much maligned *Totem and*

Taboo was an 1898 treatise by Rudolf Kleinpaul entitled *Die Lebendigen und die Toten in Volksglauben, Religion and Sage*. In that treatise which Freud praised, there is an entire section devoted to the vampire (1898:119–129). In summarizing Kleinpaul's discussion, Freud stated, "Kleinpaul believes that originally . . . the dead were all vampires, who bore ill-will towards the living, and strove to harm them and deprive them of life" (Freud 1938:853). This prompted Freud to inquire: Why do the "beloved dead" become "demons"? Is it just that the soul of the dead "envies the living" and wants to be reunited with them? His answer depended upon two premises. First, Freud contended that there is inevitably ambivalence towards the deceased loved one, that is, feelings of *both* love and hate. The latter may have involved an actual wish, albeit perhaps an unconscious one, for the death of the beloved person (1938:854). When the person dies, the survivor not surprisingly feels some guilt (for having at some point wished for the death). In some cases, the survivor may feel anger that he or she has been abandoned by the deceased. The second premise, according to Freud, is that feelings of guilt and anger on the part of the survivor are *projected* onto the deceased. In other words, "I feel anger towards the deceased" is transformed through projection into "the deceased feels anger towards me, the survivor." "Even though," said Freud, "the survivor will deny that he has ever entertained hostile impulses towards the beloved dead," the result is nonetheless the survivor's fear of being injured by a vengeful "hostile demon" (1938:855).

Freud's explanation of vampires is more fully articulated by his loyal disciple and biographer Ernest Jones, whose essay on the vampire was originally published in German in 1912, just one year before *Totem and Taboo* was published. Jones also interprets the vampire in terms of projection. The living survivors' ambivalent feelings of both love and hate (e.g., towards parents) are supposedly projected onto the deceased so that it is the corpse who feels both love and hate towards the living (1971:99–100). That is why, according to Jones, vampires frequently return to visit their nearest relatives, for example, wives, husbands, or children. Jones also suggests that the vampire belief complex involves a form of regression to an infantile "sadistic-masochistic phase of development" (1971:110). As the infant may express anger towards a parent through biting, so, through projection combined with *lex talionis*, the adult fears that the dead parent will retaliate by returning to bite him or her

(1971:112). Jones, like Freud, believed that the "hostile 'death-wishes' nourished by the child against the disturbing parent or other rival" are, after the actual death of this parent, translated through projection to a guilty conscience and a fear that the dead parental figure will return to exact vengeance (1971:112). The mixture of love and hate towards the parental figures is symbolized by sucking (love) and biting (hate), actions taken by vampires towards the living (1971:121).

The sadistic component of vampirism was noted by many writers, for example, Krafft-Ebing in his *Psychopathia Sexualis* (1953:129) and Havelock Ellis in his *Studies in the Psychology of Sex* (1928:126). But the specific hypothesis relating oral sadism to infantile conditioning came from psychoanalysis. Karl Abraham in his important 1924 paper, "The Influence of Oral Erotism on Character-Formation," described a shift from sucking to biting in the so-called oral phase of infantile development. In Abraham's words, "... the irruption of teeth ... causes a considerable part of the pleasure in sucking to be replaced by pleasure in biting" (1953:396), and in that same paper, Abraham actually speaks of "regression from the oral-sadistic to the sucking stage," which has an element of cruelty in it as well, "which makes them [such individuals] something like *vampires* to other people" (1953:401, my emphasis). Abraham's astute observation of oral phases was echoed by psychoanalyst Melanie Klein, who confirmed that "normally the infant's pleasure in sucking is succeeded by pleasure in biting" (1960:179). It is this line of reasoning which led ineluctably to such statements as "The vampire becomes a projection of oral sadism left over from the early infant-mother relationship" (Henderson 1976:610; see also Kayton 1972:310).

Melanie Klein, however, went further than her mentor Karl Abraham. It was she who postulated the critical importance of the maternal breast. She contended that an infant may, because of either overindulgence or deprivation of the maternal breast, direct aggressive impulses at that breast, its initial contact point with the mother (1960:185–186). Henderson's rendering of this situation is: "When mothering is not available at the right moment or is intruded when the infant is not reaching out for it, the breast becomes hateful and persecutory" (1976:610). Klein readily admits that this idea of an infant "trying to destroy its mother" presents a "horrifying not to say an unbelievable picture to our minds" (1960:187). The possible linkage between the "drying up of the breast" and vampirism is proposed by Copjec, who claims, "Most visual images of vampirism center on the female breast" (1991:34 n. 16).

From a folklorist perspective, we can see that, with the principle of *lex talionis*, the infant-child may fear retaliation for such aggressive impulses and that such retaliation by the parents might take the form of sucking or biting. Folklore fantasy is full of swallowing monsters who threaten to eat up children, while the "vagina dentata" (Motif F 547.1.1; see Otero 1996) could represent for males the maternal teeth threatening to bite (off) their male projection, just as male infants sought to bite (off) the projecting breast of the mother. In any event, the nursing mother confronted with oral sadistic sucking or biting on the part of a frustrated or angry infant may withdraw her breast from the infant's mouth, a perfectly reasonable course of action under the circumstances. This withdrawal of the breast would, from the infant's point of view, constitute a form of "object loss." In other words, sucking (and/or biting) the breast leads to object loss, meaning the withdrawal of the maternal breast (which in infantile logic appears to be inexhaustible: every time the infant wishes nourishment, the breast seems to be magically full again). Object loss, in general, is related to so-called separation anxiety on the part of infants, an anxiety-provoking situation which is articulated in such games as peek-a-boo and later hide-and-seek, where the "lost" object is in every case "found" and the separation anxiety alleviated (Frankiel 1993).

Now if we understand that the death of a loved one is also a form of object loss, in the psychological sense, and if there is guilt on the part of the living as having caused that death (e.g., through wishful thinking at some point), then it is possible that through projective inversion that the lost object (the deceased loved one) will return to take revenge by means of sucking or biting. This, I maintain, is precisely what we have in the folkloristic figure of the bloodsucking revenant known as the vampire.

There is another aspect of the vampire phenomenon that needs elucidation and concerns the conception of death itself. It is once again Ernest Jones who provides the critical clue. In his brilliant 1924 essay, "Psycho-Analysis and Anthropology," delivered as an address to the British Royal Anthropological Institute in February of that year, Jones suggested that death is "a reversal of the birth act leading to a return to the pre-natal existence within the maternal womb" (1951:137–138). The tomb-womb symbolic equation is now pretty much taken for granted. Freud in a footnote in his *Interpretation of Dreams* went so far as to propose that "the profoundest unconscious reason for a belief in a life after death" is "a projection into the future of this mysterious life before birth." Freud also claimed that the dread of being buried alive stems from the same prenatal experience (1938:395 n. 1). As one analyst phrases the issue, "The symbolism is obvious: Earth equals mother; coffin equals womb. The vampire is, thus, born anew each night and begins anew its search for sustaining lifeblood from another" (Henderson 1976:618).

The tomb-womb equation explains why bodies are so often buried in the fetal position. It is not to save space or work for grave-diggers, but rather to allow the corpse to assume a comfortable if not comforting position. (This also gives a rationale for why adults in pain or distress often try to sleep in the curled-up fetal position [Jones 1951:144 n. 4]). If death beliefs assume a rebirth, says Jones, then "rebirth" is really "debirth" (1951:139 n. 1). What has all this to do with vampires? I submit that, if a vampire wants to be reborn, it must do so in regressive terms, and as a newborn babe gains sustenance through sucking at its mother's breast, so a "newborn" vampire must do likewise, albeit in symbolic guise. Jones himself, in his groundbreaking essay on the vampire, quotes striking evidence supporting this hypothesis. He cites, for example, folklorist Friedrich Krauss: "Among the Southern Slavs it is believed when a Mara (there called Mora) once tastes a man's blood she falls in love with him and can never leave him. . . . she is particularly fond of sucking children's breasts" (1971:126). But despite all his insights and brilliance, here Jones unfortunately goes astray. He explains these "phantasies" as being symbols of "semen" (1971:119), an all too typical instance of the excessively male-biased interpretations so often found among early Freudians. As Stevenson points out in his 1988 *PMLA* essay on the sexuality of *Dracula*, Jones is confused. If blood is semen, how could a male vampire obtain "semen" from sucking blood *from women* (1988:146)? But Stevenson in turn is also confused when he perceives that Dracula's attack on Mina seems to be a mother engaged in breast-feeding. In this climactic and startling episode in the novel, Dracula, one may recall, forces Mina to suck *his* breast. "What is going on!" Stevenson asks, "Fellatio? Lactation?

It seems the vampire is sexually capable of anything" (1988:146). Bierman calls it "a thinly disguised primal scene in oral terms" (1972:194).

The answer at this point should be obvious. The fact that the vampire sucks milk from children's breasts, for example, could easily be construed as a perfect reversal of the initial infantile prototype. Instead of infants sucking from adult breasts, adults suckle from children's breasts. We know very well from our own Judeo-Christian eschatologial cosmology that heaven, the promised land after death, offers "milk and honey," an old-fashioned form of sweetened milk offered to infants. The idiom of "a land flowing with milk and honey" as a metaphor for abundance occurs no fewer than twenty-one times in the Bible (Beck and Smedley 1971:167). And what are we to make of the phrase "and the hills shall flow with milk" (Joel 3:18)? The only hills that flow with milk are maternal breasts. So the idea of a blissful death involving a regression to a postnatal paradise including lots of milk and honey is seemingly consonant with Judeo-Christian worldview.

Now we can better understand why the dead are thirsty. The life-giving liquid can be water, blood, or milk, among other choices. This is why the vampire is said to "suck" fluids from its victims. Sucking is the initial infantile response to the maternal breast, which according to Melanie Klein is the infant's "first object relation" (1957:3). Biting comes later (as it does in literary versions of the vampire plot) with a marked increase in oral sadism. As we've noted, the infant's teeth are its first weapon against the maternal breast. Just as the infant may want to suck the living (breast) dry, so the deceased is imagined as wanting to return to suck the living dry. Just as an infant appears to have an insatiable appetite or thirst for milk, so the vampire constantly has to seek more liquid refreshment or sustenance. However, whereas the maternal breast to the infant seems to be a magical, inexhaustible source of nutriment, the living victims of the vampires are not. When they lose their vital fluids, they themselves become vampires in need of liquid replacement. Whether this is simply a folk recognition of the communicable nature of infectious diseases, or whether it is merely an affirmation of the principle of "limited good" (Foster 1965), the end result is the same. In the latter case, if there is a finite amount of liquid "good," the vampire's gain is automatically the victim's loss. More important, by sucking on the victim, the vampire may be said to *merge* with the victim (Kayton 1972:310), which would constitute a veritable replication of the prototypic infantile breast-feeding scenario. The victim then becomes a vampire, that is, also regresses to an oral sadistic infantile level.

I believe the theory of vampires here proposed has the advantage of explaining a good many puzzling details about the vampire belief complex. We can now understand why vampires are thirsty: they are thirsty because all the dead in the Indo-European and Semitic world are considered to be thirsty, not just vampires. They are thirsty because death is debirth; the transit to the other world is the reverse of the birth process, that is, the movement through the birth canal. To be reborn, the deceased must undo death, that is, be born again. If death is truly debirth, then reversing the death process would be equivalent to rebirth. It is almost mathematical. Death is the negation of life, but the negation of death is once again life. Minus a minus equals a plus! Being born again leads to a symbolic reinstatement of the initial nurturing process, that is, the reestablishment of the first object relationship: sucking the maternal breast. But as the dead are angry (at being dead—or so the living suppose), the sucking is quite vicious; the dead suck their victims to death. We can now also understand why the vampire attacks members of its own immediate family, and also why the vampire is said to sometimes attack cows and goats, obvious milk-giving substitutes for the original maternal breast. We can now better appreciate the various apotropaic measures employed to prevent vampires from carrying out their nefarious actions. Burning a corpse, like cremation, completes the desiccating process (see Čajkanović 1974). Once *all* the liquid is removed, the corpse is permanently dead. Decapitation is also effective because, if the deceased has no mouth, it cannot possibly mount an oral attack on the breast. Driving a stake through the purported vampire's heart is not an attempt to pinion the corpse by impalement, but rather an efficacious means of draining the last remaining liquid (blood) from it, which like burning or cremation completes the dessicating death of the only partly deceased.

The oral erotic basis of vampirism would also help explain why this belief complex can so easily serve as a convenient metaphor for adult sexuality ranging from "normal" oedipal heterosexuality (in many literary texts, the vampire typically attacks a member of the opposite sex) to homosexuality (Dyer 1988) and lesbianism (Case 1991; see also Melton

1994:301–302, 362–366; and Gordon and Hollinger 1997). The latter forms of sexuality, after all, often do involve oral-genital sucking activity. For that matter, even kissing is essentially an act of sucking, not to mention the "love-bite" (Morse 1993:193).

Finally, it is my contention that it is the underlying oral erotic basis of the vampire belief complex which partly explains the endless fascination of this enigmatic creature. In prudish Victorian times, the Bram Stoker novel provided a much-needed outlet for repressed sexuality (see Bentley 1972; Stevenson 1988), but even in the twentieth century, the vampire of popular culture and literature serves a similar function. The fear of being attacked by a vampire—at night, in one's own bedroom—can be construed as a form of wishful thinking. The vampire in the grave is analogous to a sleeping parent. It is an incarnate expression of a child's ambivalence towards his or her parent of the opposite sex. While the initial sucking of the breast can be an expression of love, too much sucking (or certainly biting) can be an act of aggression. The vampire, though overtly carrying out an aggressive act, also approximates the original life-giving and partly erotic breast-feeding relationship. That is why the vampire is both feared and regarded as fascinating, even to young children watching vampire movies on television or vampires in animated cartoons.

In conclusion, we can now argue that the theory of the origin of the word *vampire*, which suggested that the term comes from a root *pī*, meaning "to drink," makes perfectly good sense. Drinking, or rather sucking, is an essential sine qua non of vampirism. And this is so even if one cannot accept the proposed infantile origin of this remarkable living legend, which will never die as long as it can continue to renew itself with future generations yet unborn.

References Cited

Abraham, K. 1953. "The Influence of Oral Erotism on Character-Formation." In Karl Abraham, *Selected Papers on Psychoanalysis*, 393–406. New York: Basic Books.
Afanas'ev, A. N. 1976. "Poetic Views of the Slavs Regarding Nature." In *Vampires of the Slavs*, ed. Jan L. Perkowski, 160–170. Cambridge: Slavica Publishers.
Anon. 1950. "Vampire." In *Standard Dictionary of Folklore, Mythology, and Legend*, ed. Maria Leach, 1154. New York: Funk & Wagnalls.
Barber, P. 1987. "Forensic Pathology and the European Vampire." *Journal of Folklore Research* 24:1–32.
Barber, P. 1988. *Vampires, Burial, and Death: Folklore and Reality*. New Haven: Yale University Press.

30   The Vampire as Bloodthirsty Revenant

Beck, B. F., and D. Smedley. 1971. *Honey and Your Health*. New York: Bantam.
Bellucci, G. 1909. "Sul bisogno di dissetarsi attribuito all'anima dei morti." *Archivio per l'antropologia e la etnolgia* 39:211–229.
Bent, J. T. 1886. "On Insular Greek Customs." *Journal of the Anthropological Institute* 15:391–403.
Bentley, C. F. 1972. "The Monster in the Bedroom: Sexual Symbolism in Bram Stoker's *Dracula*" *Literature and Psychology* 22:27–34.
Beynen, G. K. 1988. "The Vampire in Bulgarian Folklore." *Vtori Mezhdunaroken Kongres po bulgarestika*, 456–465. Sofia.
Bielfeldt, H. K. 1971. "Die Wortgeschichte von Deutsch *Vampir* und *Vamp*." In *Serta Slavica in Memoriam Aloisii Schmaus*, 42–47. Munich: Rudolf Trofenik.
Bierman, J. 1972. "Dracula: Prolonged Childhood Illness and the Oral Triad." *American Imago* 29:186–198.
Bourguignon, A. 1997. "Vampirism and Autovampirism." In *Sexual Dynamics of Anti-Social Behavior*, ed. Louis B. Schlesinger and Eugene Revitch, 271–293. 2nd ed. Springfield: Charles C. Thomas.
Buck, C. D. 1949. *A Dictionary of Selected Synonyms in the Principal Indo-European Languages*. Chicago: University of Chicago Press.
Burkhart, D. 1966. "Vampirglaube und Vampirsage auf dem Balkan." In Alois Schmaus, ed., *Beiträge zur Südosteuropa-Forschung*, ed. Alois Schmaus, 211–252. Munich: Rudolf Trofenik.
Čajkanović, V. 1974. "The Killing of a Vampire." *Folklore Forum* 7: 260-271.
Carter, M. L. 1989. *The Vampire in Literature: A Bibliography*. Ann Arbor: UMI Research Press.
Case, S.-E. 1991. "Tracking the Vampire." *Differences: A Journal of Feminist Cultural Studies* 3(2): 1–20.
Chotjewitz, P. O. 1968. "Der Vampir: Theorie und Kritik einer Mythe." *Merkur* 8:708–719.
Copjec, J. 1991. "Vampires, Breast-Feeding, and Anxiety." *October* 58:25–43.
Cremene, A. 1981. *La Mythologie du vampire en Roumanie*. Monaco: Éditions du Rocher.
Deonna, W. 1939. "Croyances Funeraires: La soif des morts; le mort musicien." *Revue de l'histoire des religions* 119:53–81.
Djordjević, T. R. 1953. ["Vampires in the Folk Beliefs of Our People"]. (in Serbian). *Recueil Serbe d'ethnographie* 66:149–219.
du Boulay, J. 1982. "The Greek Vampire: A Study of Cyclic Symbolism in Marriage and Death." *Man* 17:219–238.
Dundes, A. 1980. *Interpreting Folklore*. Bloomington: Indiana University Press.
Durham, E. 1923. "Of Magic, Witches and Vampires in the Balkans." *Man* 23: 189–192.
Dyer, R. 1988. "Children of the Night: Vampirism as Homosexuality, Homosexuality as Vampirism." In *Sweet Dreams: Sexuality, Gender, and Popular Fiction*, ed. Susannah Radstone, 47–72. London: Lawrence & Wishart.
Ellis, H. 1928. *Studies in the Psychology of Sex*. Vol. 3. Philadelphia: F. A. Davis.
Fischer, A. 1927. "Upior, strzgon czy wieszczy?" *Lud* 26:84.
Florescu, R. 1985–86. "The Dracula Search in Retrospect." *New England Social Studies Bulletin* 43:25–50.
Foster, G. 1965. "Peasant Society and the Image of Limited Good." *American Anthropologist* 67:293–315.
Frankiel, R. V. 1993. "Hide-and-Seek in the Playroom: On Object Loss and Transference in Child Treatment." *Psychoanalytic Review* 80:341–359.
Freud, S. 1938. *The Basic Writings of Sigmund Freud*. New York: Modern Library.
Frost, B. J. 1989. *The Monster with A Thousand Faces: Guises of the Vampire in Myth and Literature*. Bowling Green: Bowling Green State University Popular Press.
Gelder, K. 1994. *Reading the Vampire*. London: Routledge.
Gordon, J., and V. Hollinger, eds. 1997. *Blood Read: The Vampire as Metaphor in Contemporary Culture*. Philadelphia: University of Pennsylvania Press.
Gottlieb, R. M. 1991. "The European Vampire: Applied Psychoanalysis and Applied Legend." *Folklore Forum* 24:39–61.

Gottlieb, R. M. 1994. "The Legend of the European Vampire: Object Loss and Corporeal Preservation." *Psychoanalytic Study of the Child* 49:465–480.
Grimm, J. 1966. *Teutonic Mythology*. Vol. 4. New York: Dover.
Hanush, J. J. 1859. "Die Vampyre." *Zeitschrift für Deutsche Mythologie und Sittenkunde* 4:198–201.
Henderson, D. J. 1976. "Exorcism, Possession, and the Dracula Cult: A Synopsis of Object-Relations Psychology." *Bulletin of the Menninger Clinic* 40:603–628.
Jaffé, P. D., and F. DiCataldo. 1994. "Clinical Vampirism: Blending Myth and Reality." *Bulletin of the American Academy of Psychiatry and the Law* 22:533–544.
Jaworskij, J. 1898. Südrussiche Vampyre. *Zeitschrift des Vereins für Volkskunde* 8:331–335.
Jellinek, A. L. 1904. "Zur Vampyrsage." *Zeitschrift des Vereins für Volkskunde* 14:322–328.
Jones, E. 1951. "Psycho-Analysis and Anthropology." In Ernest Jones, *Essays in Applied Psychoanalysis*, 114–144. Vol. 2 of *Essays in Folklore, Anthropology and Religion*. London: Hogarth press.
Jones, E. 1971. *On the Nightmare*. New York: Liveright.
Kayton, L. 1972. "The Relationship of the Vampire Legend to Schizophrenia." *Journal of Youth and Adolescence* 1:303–314.
Klein, M. 1957. *Envy and Gratitude: A Study of Unconscious Sources*. New York: Basic Books.
Klein, M. 1960. *The Psychoanalysis of Children*. New York: Grove Press.
Kleinpaul, R. 1898. *Die Lebendigen und die Toten in Volksglauben, Religion und Sage*. Leipzig: G. J. Göschen.
Krafft-Ebing, R. v. 1953. *Psychopathia Sexualis*. New York: Pioneer Publications.
Krauss, F. S. 1892a. "Vampyre in südslawischen Volksglauben." *Globus* 61:325–328.
Krauss, F. S. 1892b. "Südslawische Schutzmittel gegen Vampyre." *Globus* 62:203–204.
Leatherdale, C. 1985. *Dracula: The Novel & the Legend*. Wellingborough: Aquarian Press.
Lloyd, G. E. R. 1964. "The Hot and the Cold, the Dry and the Wet in Greek Philosophy." *Journal of Hellenic Studies* 84:92–106.
Mannhardt, W. 1859. "Über Vampyrismus." *Zeitschrift für Deutsche Mythologie und Sittenkunde* 4:259–282.
Marigny, J. 1985. *Le Vampire dans la littérature anglo-saxonne*. 2 vols. Paris: Didier Érudition.
Marigny, J. 1986. "La tradition légendaire du vampire en Europe." *Les Cahiers du G.E.R.F.* 1:165–186.
Melton, J. G. 1994. *The Vampire Book: The Encyclopedia of the Undead*. Detroit: Visible Ink Press.
Morse, D. R. 1993. "The Stressful Kiss: A Biopsychosocial Evaluation of the Origins, Evolution, and Societal Significance of Vampirism." *Stress Medicine* 9:181–199.
Murgoci, A. 1926. "The Vampire in Roumania." *Folklore* 86:320–349.
Naylor, K. E. 1983. "The Source of the Word 'Vampir' in Slavic." *Southeastern Europe* 10:93–98.
Nixon, D. 1979. "Vampire Lore and Alleged Cases." *Miorita* 6:14–28.
Oinas, F. 1978. "Heretics as Vampires and Demons in Russia." *Slavic and East European Journal* 22:433–441.
Oinas, F. 1982. "East Euroepan Vampires & Dracula." *Journal of Popular Culture* 16:108–116.
Onians, R. B. 1973. *The Origins of European Thought*. New York: Arno Press.
Otero, S. 1996. " 'Fearing Our Mothers': An Overview of the Psychoanalytic Theories Concerning the Vagina Dentata Motif F 547.1.1." *American Journal of Psychoanalysis* 56:269–288.
Perkowski, J. L. 1976. *Vampires of the Slavs*. Cambridge: Slavica Publishers.
Perkowski, J. L. 1982. "The Romanian Folkloric Vampire." *East European Quarterly* 16:311–322.
Perkowski, J. L. 1989. *The Darkling: A Treatise on Slavic Vampirism*. Columbus, Ohio: Slavica Publishers.
Perkowski, J. L. 1992a. *Cats, Bats, and Vampires*. New York: Dracula Press.
Perkowski, J. L. 1992b. *Daemon Contamination Balkan Vampire Lore*. New York: Dracula Press.
Politis, N. G. 1894. "On the Breaking of Vessels as Funeral Rite in Modern Greece." *Journal of the Royal Anthropological Institute* 23:28–41.
Polívka, G. 1901. "Über das Wort 'Vampyr'." *Zeitschrift für österreichische Volkskunde* 7:185.

Popov, Rachko. 1983. "Vampirut bulgarskite narodni viarvaniia." (The Vampire in Bulgarian Folk Beliefs). *Vekove* 9:36–43.
Prins, H. 1984. "Vampirism—Legendary or Clinical Phenomenon." *Medicine, Science and the Law* 24:283–293.
Prins, H. 1885. "Vampirism—a Clinical Condition." *British Journal of Psychiatry* 146:666–668.
Riccardo, M. V. 1983. *Vampires Unearthed: The Complete Multimedia Vampire & Dracula Bibliography*. New York: Garland.
Ryan, J. S. 1993. "The Vampire before and after Stoker's *Dracula*." *Contemporary Legend* 3:145–154.
Sartori, P. 1908. "Das Wasser im Totengebrauche." *Zeitschrift des Vereins für Volkskunde* 18:253–378.
Schierup, C.-U. 1986. "Why Are Vampires Still Alive? Wallachian Immigrants in Scandinavia." *Ethnos* 51:173–198.
Senn, H. A. 1982. *Were-Wolf and Vampire in Romania*. Boulder: East European Quarterly.
Shanahan, M. L. 1985. "Psychoanalytical Approaches." In C. Leatherdale, *Dracula: The Novel & the Legend*, 160–175. Wellingborough: Aquarian Press.
Shanahan, M. L. 1994. "Psychological Perspectives on Vampire Mythology." In *The Vampire Book: The Encyclopedia of the Undead*, ed. J. G. Melton, 492–501. Detroit: Visible Ink Press.
Stevenson, J. A. 1988. "A Vampire in the Mirror: The Sexuality of Dracula." *PMLA* 103:139–149.
Summers, M. 1995. *The Vampire*. London: Senate.
Summers, M. 1996. *The Vampire in Europe*. London: Bracken Books.
Thompson, S. 1955–1958. *The Motif-Index of Folk-Literature*. 6 vols. Bloomington: Indiana University Press.
Twitchell, J. 1980. "The Vampire Myth." *American Imago* 37:83–92.
Vanden Bergh, R. L., and J. F. Kelly. 1964. "Vampirism: A Review with New Observations." *Archives of General Psychiatry* 11:543–547.
Vukanović, T. P. 1957–59. "The Vampire." *Journal of the Gypsy Lore Society* 36:125–131; 37:21–31, 111–118; 38:44–55.
Weslowski, E. 1910. "Die Vampirsage im rumánischen Volksglauben." *Zeitschrift für österreichische Volkskunde* 16:209–216.
Wilson, K. M. 1985. "The History of the Word 'Vampire'." *Journal of the History of Ideas* 46:577–583.
Wollmann, F. 1920–23. "Vampyrické pověsti v oblasti středo-Evropské." *Naradopisný věstnik českoslavaksky* 14(1):1–16; 14(2): 1–57; 15(1):1–58; 16:80–96, 133–149; 18:133–161.
Yvonneau, M. 1990. "Matricide et vampirisme." *L'Evolution Psychiatrique* 55:575–585.

3

Projective Inversion in the Ancient Egyptian "Tale of Two Brothers"

In 1852, the text of an ancient Egyptian folktale, written on papyrus, known as the "Tale of Two Brothers" was first revealed to the scholarly community. This tale has been called, rightly or wrongly, "The Oldest Fairy Tale in the World" (Hollis 1990). However, it is certainly not the oldest recorded folktale (Jason and Kempinski 1981). Not surprisingly, it has attracted the notice of many of the leading folklorists of the nineteenth and twentieth centuries, notably Mannhardt (1859), Cosquin (1877), Lang (1899:2:317–29) and Von Sydow (1930), among others. The abundant folkloristic scholarship (not to mention that of the Egyptologists) is ably surveyed by the Czech folklorist Karel Horálek in his entry devoted to "Brüdermärchen: Das ägyptische" in the *Enzyklopädie des Märchens* (1978b) and especially by Susan Hollis in her Harvard doctoral dissertation that examined the tale and its likely original Egyptian context in great depth (1990).

One reason for the great interest in the tale was its undoubted antiquity. It appears to have been recorded in the thirteenth century before the Christian era, which would make it more than three millennia old. The great Swedish folklorist Von Sydow observed that the survival of the tale into the twentieth century "shows that a tale can live for more than 3000 years unsupported by written literature" (1948:32). Another reason that folklorists have been fascinated by the tale is the numerous traditional motifs that it contains. For the convenience of the reader, let me

34 Projective Inversion in "Tale of Two Brothers"

first give a synopsis of the tale based on the full text provided by Hollis (1990:5–15).

Two brothers, Anubis and Bata, live together along with the wife of Anubis, who is unnamed. One day when the younger brother Bata returns to the house, the wife of Anubis tries to seduce him, saying, "Come, let us spend an hour lying down." Bata became angry "because of the evil word she said to him," and he replied, "Now see, you are like a mother to me. Further, your husband is like a father to me. Now the one older than I, he has raised me." Later Anubis returns, and the spurned wife, fearful that Bata might tell him of her attempted infidelity, put on grease markings to give the appearance of having been beaten. When Anubis asked about this, she claimed that she had been beaten by Bata after she rebuffed his attempt to seduce her (Motif K 2111, Potiphar's Wife). She claimed to have told Bata, "Now, am I not your mother? Further, your older brother is like a father to you." The wife then asks Anubis to kill Bata: "Now if you let him live, I will die." Anubis goes to the stable and hides behind the door, prepared to kill his brother, but a helpful cow warns Bata in time for him to escape (Motif B 211, Advice from a Speaking Cow). Bata prays to the Sun God for help, and a river full of crocodiles appears, separating him from Anubis in pursuit (Motif D 672, Obstacle Flight). Bata then tells Anubis what really happened and chastises him for taking the word of a "filthy whore" without even hearing his side of the matter. Bata then takes a "reed knife and he cut off his phallus (Motif S 176.1, Mutilation: emasculation), and he threw it to the water and a wels fish swallowed it."

Bata then directs his brother to go home after informing him that he has cut out his heart and placed it "on the top of the blossom of the pine" (Motif E 712.1, Soul hidden in tree, Motif E 714.4, Soul [life] in the heart). Bata also says that if the tree is cut down, his brother should come find his heart and place it in a bowl of cool water. The brother will know that Bata is in trouble when a jug of beer suddenly foams (Motif E 761.6.4, Life token: beer foams). Anubis returns home and kills his wife, throwing her body to the dogs.

Meanwhile, Bata goes to the Valley of the Pine where the gods create a beautiful woman to be his companion/wife. He warns her to keep away from the sea, as he could not save her inasmuch as his heart has been placed on top of the flower of the pine. She disobeys and a plait of her hair is carried by the sea to Egypt where the washermen of the Pharaoh wash his clothes. The odor of the plait permeates the clothing and causes the Pharaoh to fall in love. The plait of hair is brought to him and he orders a search party to seek the woman in question (Motif T11.4.1, Love through sight of hair of unknown princess). The woman is brought to the Pharaoh, who marries her. He asks her about her previous husband, and she tells him to "Have the pine cut and have it destroyed" (Motif K 2213.4, Betrayal of Husband's Secret by his Wife). This act kills Bata.

Anubis notices foam on his jug of beer, and he goes in search of his younger brother. He finds Bata's heart, puts it in cool water, and Bata comes back to life (Motif E 30 Resuscitation by arrangement of members, Motif E 125.3, Resuscitation by brother). Bata then transforms himself into a bull (Motif E 611.2.1, Reincarnation as bull) and asks his brother to take him to the Pharaoh. As a bull, he reveals to the Pharaoh's wife that he has become alive again (Motif E 670, Repeated reincarnation). Once again she betrays Bata by demanding that the Pharaoh slay the bull so that she can eat its liver. When the bull is slaughtered, two drops of blood fall, one on each side of the Pharaoh's entrance door. The drops of blood grow into "two great persea trees." Again, Bata in the form of the trees foolishly tells the Pharaoh's wife of his new identity, whereupon she succeeds in convincing the Pharaoh to cut down the two trees to make furniture. In the process of cutting down the trees, "a splinter flew and it entered the mouth of the noblewoman, and then she swallowed it, and she became pregnant." Later she gives birth to a son who is Bata (Motif E 607.2, Person transforms self, is swallowed and reborn in new form). The Pharaoh is delighted with his son and appoints him as ruler of the whole land. Later after the Pharaoh dies, Bata becomes king and calls for an assembly of all the officials to serve as a jury. He condemns the Pharaoh's wife for her misdeeds, and the "jury" concurs in the judgment. Bata then summons his older brother Anubis. After ruling for thirty years, Bata dies and is succeeded on the throne by Anubis.

Stith Thompson, arguably the greatest American folklorist of the twentieth century, was struck by the large number of traditional motifs contained in the tale. In his classic book *The Folktale* he remarked, "It is of great interest to the student of oral fiction to know that at least these themes were already developed as early as the thirteenth century before Christ" (1946:276). It is noteworthy that Thompson in his summary of the tale's plot (275) fails to include Bata's self-emasculation, an omission noted by Hollis (1990:187n70). Nor is this critical motif mentioned in Thompson's description of tale type 318, The Faithless Wife, the tale type he assigns to the Egyptian tale of two brothers (Aarne and Thompson 1961:112). Thompson's prudishness comes as no surprise when one recalls that he bothered to write a special footnote to his entry Motif X 700, Humor concerning sex. In what was supposed to be a comprehensive six-volume worldwide listing of folk narrative motifs, he doesn't list so much as a single bibliographical citation for this category. The footnote offers the following lame excuse for this omission: "Thousands of obscene motifs in which there is no point except the obscenity itself might logically come at this point, but they are entirely beyond the scope of the present work" (1955–58:5:541n1). As a sop, Thompson says that he is leaving the space X 700 to X 749 free in case someone someday might possibly want to classify such motifs. Did Thompson really imagine that fifty numerical motif slots could possibly accommodate "thousands of obscene motifs"? In a field such as folklore, it is unforgivable for a scholar to indulge in such self-imposed censorship. In this context, it is perhaps understandable why Thompson elected to leave out the motif of self-castration in the Egyptian tale of two brothers!

From the very beginning of the scholarly fascination with the tale of two brothers, it was clearly the Potiphar's Wife motif that attracted the most attention. A central part of the story of Joseph in Genesis, this motif caused folklorists to remark upon the striking plot similarity between the two narratives. Joseph was a slave in Potiphar's household, and when Potiphar's wife tried repeatedly to seduce him but was unsuccessful, she accused Joseph of having tried to seduce her. Potiphar believed his wife and put Joseph into prison (Genesis 39). The motif has widespread distribution. Yohannan, the editor of *Joseph and Potiphar's Wife in World Literature*, comments, "One would be hard put to find a story that has had a wider circulation among more varied audiences over a longer period of time than this one" (1968:1). The considerable scholarship devoted to this motif includes Faverty (1931), Hollis (1989), Aycock (1992), and Goldman (1995). The antiquity of the motif in India, for example, is attested by the fact that it occurs in a Jataka tale (Bloomfield 1923, Grey 1990:66–68; 1998:118). (For Arabic texts, see the references listed for Motif 2111 in El-Shamy 1995:1:260.)

For anyone the least bit familiar with the history of folkloristics, it should come as no surprise to learn that the initial folkloristic considerations of the tale of two brothers were concerned with adducing parallels to particular motifs contained in the tale and to speculating about the possible origins of the tale. In the nineteenth century, one of the governing intellectual paradigms was the search for origins. (For a detailed account of the various folkloristic studies of the tale, see Hollis 1990:16–48; for a discussion of other ancient Egyptian wonder tales, see Hollis 1995.) A particularly popular origin theory of folktales in general was that they had diffused to the Near East and Europe from India. Opponents of this Indianist theory were thrilled with the discovery of the Egyptian tale of two brothers. Andrew Lang's remark is perhaps typical. Early in his discussion of the tale, Lang comments: "We ask no more than this one *märchen* of ancient Egypt to upset the whole theory that India was the original home of the *contes,* and that from *historic* India they have been carried by oral transmission and in literary vehicles all over the world" (1899:2:318). Lang continues, "Even a hasty examination of these incidents from old Egypt proves that before India was heard of in history, the people of the Pharaohs possessed a large store of incidents perfectly familiar in modern *märchen* . . . What we do know is, that if we find a large share of the whole stock of incident of popular tale fully developed in one single story long before India was historic, it is perfectly vain to argue that all stories were imported from historic India" (2:326, 327). Lang's comment was echoed in the next century by Von Sydow: "This tale, then, is an incontrovertible argument against the theory that all tales should have originated in India" (1948:33).

In the twentieth century, the emphasis in folkloristics shifted from concerns with origins to an interest in classification and typology. This was in part a general movement away from diachronic approaches to synchronic ones. Accordingly, there was much less hunting for motif parallels and debating about whether folktales may or may not have diffused from India. Instead, discussion centered on whether the tale of two brothers was a myth or a folktale, or if a folktale, to what tale type did it belong? The suggestion that it was a myth depended upon the premise that Bata was a reflex of the Egyptian god Osiris and that stories about gods were myths, not folktales. Dutch folklorist Jan de Vries, for example, insisted that the tale was a myth, not a folktale (1954:51, 60). This is, of course, a totally fallacious bit of reasoning. Folk narrative genres are not dependent upon the identity of *dramatis personae*. Gods may be characters in myths, folktales, and legends. Hence the presence of a god in a narrative provides no indication whatsoever of the generic nature of the narrative. A myth is a sacred narrative explaining how the world and humankind came to be as they are. In that light, it is obvious that the Egyptian tale of two brothers is definitely not a myth. It is almost certainly a folktale, and within the folktale rubric, it bears the unquestionable characteristics of a wonder or fairy tale.

Most folklorists agree that the narrative is a wonder tale. Von Sydow, for instance, used the tale as an example of his important concept of oicotype or local/regional variant. Drawing from his essay (1930) devoted to the tale, Von Sydow distinguished two basic oicotypes: the Slavonic and the Indo-Persian (1948:32). Horalek has sought to refine Von Sydow's distinctions by discussing "European" and "Asiatic" forms of the tale (1964b:31, 1968, 1978b:235). But much of the debate concerning classification has to do with tale typology. To what tale type does the tale of two brothers belong? Aarne did not include it in his original 1910 *Verzeichnis der Märchentypen*. Nor did Stith Thompson add it in his 1928 revision of Aarne's index. But in the 1961 revision, Thompson did add type 318, The Faithless Wife. Batu: the Egyptian "Two Brothers" Tale. Thompson is nothing if not consistent and therefore we should not be in the least surprised that the plot summary for Aarne-Thompson tale type 318 makes no mention of the self-emasculation motif.

The problem with respect to tale typology stems from the fact that the Egyptian tale contains motifs found in other tale types. For instance, the life token motif (E 761) is also found in Aarne-Thompson tale type 303, The Twins or Blood Brothers, while the external soul motif is found in Aarne-Thompson tale type 302, The Ogre's (Devil's) Heart in the Egg. The late Anna Birgitta Rooth in her doctoral dissertation devoted to Cinderella, written under her mentor Von Sydow's direction, discussed several motifs contained in the Egyptian tale. One is "The tress of hair which floats away on the water" that "falls into the king's hands with the result that the king is seized with a desire to find the owner" who "is the wife of the hero" (1951:70). Rooth notes, correctly, that this motif is contained in Aarne-Thompson tale type 590A, The Treacherous Wife, a tale type that Horalek persuasively argues is equivalent if not identical to Aarne-

Thompson tale type 318, The Faithless Wife (Horalek 1978b:925). In other words, Aarne-Thompson 318 and 590A are in effect the same tale. Horalek also indicates the relevance of Aarne-Thompson tale type 516B, The Abducted Princess (Love Through Sight of Floating Hair), a tale which is apparently primarily found in India. Rooth also discussed the motif of the "stepmother who pretends to be ill and demands the liver or flesh of the animal to eat" (1951:140) and specifically compares it to the Egyptian tale of the two brothers. This motif is found in Aarne-Thompson tale type 511A, The Little Red Ox. Jason and Kempinski in their comprehensive survey of ancient folktales consider the tale of two brothers to be a combination of Aarne-Thompson tale types 303, 516B and 590A with no mention of 318 (1981:6). It is not my intent to attempt to unravel all the complexities of the debate about which tale type number or numbers are the most appropriate to identify the Egyptian tale of two brothers. (For a representative sample of the debate, see Horalek 1978a:258n1.) I mention the above details only to demonstrate the abiding interest among twentieth-century folklorists in the endless discussion of classificatory matters.

This admittedly cursory summary of some of the highlights of the nineteenth- and twentieth-century folkloristic scholarship devoted to the Egyptian tale of the two brothers demonstrates both the strengths and weaknesses of folkloristics generally. Praiseworthy is surely the insistence upon the comparative method even if the laudable goal of establishing a probable or possible origin of an item of folklore remains elusive and essentially unattainable. The obsession with classification is understandable in the light of pressing practical needs with respect to archiving and to bringing order to huge masses of collected field data. What is perhaps most disappointing and disturbing is the virtual lack of any concerted effort on the part of folklorists to speculate about the likely meaning or meanings of the tale. The hint of mother-son incest combined with an overt act of self-emasculation, one would think, might have encouraged at least one folklorist to speculate about why the tale existed in the first place (and why it was thought worthwhile to have been recorded). But such does not seem to be the case.

The problem may be couched by means of an analogy. If the fairy tale, as a genre, were perceived as a dream, then a fairy tale would consist of at least two levels of content: the manifest content and the latent content. The manifest content of a fairy tale would be the literal sequence of actions in the narrative while the latent content would be the tale's underlying symbolic (and unconscious) structure. Unfortunately, most folklorists tend to be literal-minded to a fault and they absolutely reject out of hand any possibility of there being a symbolic or psychological structure at the base of fairy tales. A couple of representative examples can stand for many. N. M. Penzer's extensive note on "Women Whose Love Is Scorned" in which he discusses the Potiphar's Wife motif (and also the Egyptian tale of two brothers) has this to say: "The whole point of the *motif* is, I feel, the refusal of the man and the consequent intended revenge of the woman" (1924:2:122). This constitutes a wholly literal reading of the first part of the tale. Equally literal is a Russian scholar's reading of the tale of two brothers that insists "The folktale asserts the morality of the patriarchal family, emphasizing the importance of friendship between the brothers, at the same time demonstrating that a wife who is unfaithful or who betrays her husband must die" (Mat'e 1964:42).

In my opinion, the latent content of the Egyptian tale of two brothers cannot possibly be understood without recourse to the psychoanalytic concepts of projection and projective inversion. In view of folklorists' traditional hostility to psychoanalytic reasoning, let me briefly describe these two critical concepts. Let me first discuss simple or pure projection. This is a process whereby an individual's thoughts or emotions are cast upon a convenient screen. An elementary example in folklore would be the various constellations of stars. If one imagines for the sake of argument that all the visible stars are dots, then one could perceive different cultures' constellations as varying ways of connecting those dots into various gestalts.

Constellations not only have different names in different cultures but very often they serve as permanent mnemonic reminders of mythological narratives. In other words, essentially human acts of love and war are translated or rather projected onto a heavenly screen. The Western placement of the planet Earth between Venus (love) and Mars (war) would be an example of such projection. The planets, after all, were not created with names. It is we humans, at least in the West, who have given them these names.

A more earthbound example of projection in folklore would be the widespread genre of the shadow play in which a light projects the shadows of puppet figures onto a screen. Moreover, when anthropologist Clifford Geertz's Javanese elementary school teacher informant told him that "the main purpose of the *wajang* [shadow play] was to draw a picture of inner thought and feeling, to give external form to internal feeling" (Geertz 1968:312) we have a remarkable confirmation of Freud's insight that "a large portion of the mythological conception of the world which reaches far into the most modern religions, is *nothing but psychology projected to the outer world*" (1938:164). This notion, which appeared in *The Psychopathology of Everyday Life,* first published in 1901 was prefigured in one of Freud's letters to his pen pal Wilhelm Fliess. In a letter of 12 December 1897, Freud wrote "Can you imagine what 'endopsychic myths' are? The latest product of my mental labor. The dim inner perception of one's own psychic apparatus stimulates thought illusions, which of course are projected onto the outside and characteristically, into the future and the beyond . . . Psycho-mythology" (Freud 1985:286).

We are here concerned not with the genre of myth but of folktale. And in this context, perhaps the most striking illustration of the Freudian concept of projection is provided by the tale of Oedipus. Freud's first articulation of this now famous example came once again in one of his letters to Fliess. In his letter of 15 October 1897, Freud spoke about how difficult it was to carry out a self-analysis. "It is by no means easy. Being totally honest with oneself is a good exercise. A single idea of general value dawned on me. I have found, in my own case too, [the phenomenon of] being in love with my mother and jealous of my father, and I now consider it a universal event in early childhood . . . If this is so, we can understand the gripping power of *Oedipus Rex* . . . the Greek legend seizes upon a compulsion which everyone recognizes because he senses its existence within himself" (1985:272). Freud was disappointed in Fliess's evident lack of response to this insight. In Freud's letter of 5 November 1897, he complains, "You said nothing about my interpretation of *Oedipus Rex* . . . Since I have not told it to anyone else, because I can well imagine in advance the bewildered rejection, I should like to have a short comment on it from you" (277).

Fortunately, Freud had the courage of his convictions, and in 1900, he published his insight in *The Interpretation of Dreams.*

> According to my already extensive experience, parents play a leading part in the infantile psychology of all persons... Falling in love with one parent and hating the other forms part of the permanent stock of the psychic impulses which arise in early childhood... Antiquity has furnished us with legendary matter which corroborates this belief... I am referring to the legend of King Oedipus and the *Oedipus Rex* of Sophocles... There must be a voice within us which is prepared to acknowledge the compelling power of fate in the *Oedipus*... His fate moves us only because it might have been our own... It may be that we were all destined to direct our first sexual impulses toward our mothers, and our first impulses of hatred and violence toward our fathers... King Oedipus, who slew his father Laius and wedded his mother Jocasta, is nothing more or less than a wish-fulfillment—the fulfillment of the wish of our childhood. (1938:306–8)

Freud's labeling of the Oedipus plot as a legend is not accurate, technically speaking, but since Aarne's tale type index in which the *folktale* of Oedipus was assigned the number 931 did not appear until 1910, this is understandable. Even a century later, most psychoanalysts and others continue to wrongly refer to the Oedipus story as a myth. Had Freud been aware of the total gamut of versions of the Oedipus tale type other than the literary version penned by Sophocles, he would no doubt have been delighted. For example, there are twenty-seven versions in which the son is asked to stand guard over the orchard or garden of his mother (wife) or father. An intruder enters the garden and is killed by the son. The intruder turns out to be the son's own father (Edmunds 1985:18). If the orchard or garden represents parental property, that is, the female genital area, then the son's killing his own father who seeks to "enter" this domain *at night* makes perfect Oedipal sense. An interesting confirmation of the symbolism of the garden occurs in a medieval version of the Potiphar's Wife plot when the frustrated woman complains about Joseph to her friends: "Though I asked him to plow in my garden, he does not wish to" (Kugel 1990:32).

It is important to realize that in the case of simple straightforward projection, one has a virtually literal one-to-one relationship between the earthly plot translated to the celestial realm or the internal individual psychological trauma cast in the external form of a fairy tale. In other words, one does not have to indulge in any interpretive sleight of hand to argue that the Oedipus tale type has something to do with a young male's killing his father and marrying his mother. This is explicit in the tale.

Having sought to explain projection in folklore (see also Dundes 1980:33–61), I should now like to consider projective inversion. What, for example, is the difference between projection and projective inversion? A problem arises because of what I perceive to be some confusion in the psychoanalytic literature. On the one hand, classic or what has been termed simple projection "refers to the normal process whereby the individual misperceives the outer world as a result of inner states" (Lindzey 1961:29, Rycroft 1968:125, cf. Bellak 1944, Blankenburg 1975). On the other hand, Freud in his 1911 paper "Psycho-Analytic Notes upon an Autobiographical Account of a Case of Paranoia," claims that the "proposition 'I hate him' becomes transformed by *projection* into another one: 'He hates (persecutes) me, which will justify me in hating him'" (Freud 1959:3:449). I would prefer to call this mechanism "projective inversion." It differs from projection insofar as it involves a "reversal" (Rycroft 1968:126) or a transformation whereby subject and object exchange places. By transposing subject and object in such a thought as "I hate you," one succeeds in "blaming the victim." If I believe you hate me, then I am presumably perfectly justified in taking appropriate action against you.

Projective inversion may be clearer if we use a folkloristic example. Otto Rank in his pathbreaking *The Myth of the Birth of the Hero*, first published in 1909, a section of which was actually written by Freud (Rank 1959:67–71), suggested that the common initial motif in the hero pattern whereby the father or a father surrogate tries to kill his own son is a projection of the son's Oedipal wish to kill his father. Rank, following Freud, calls this projection (78), but I would call it "projective inversion" instead. One decided advantage of projective inversion is that the son need feel no guilt for his patricidal wish. If his father is trying to kill him, he is only acting in self-defense in their father-son combat.

Another example of possible projective inversion may be found in the Old Testament. In one of the myths of the creation of man, we are told that God created man in His own image: "So God created man in his own image, in the image of God created he him; male and female created he them" (Genesis 1:27). It would be disrespectful if not downright sacrilegious to say that "Man created God in his own image." Hence by a simple transform, we have a story of God creating man in His own image.

In female-centered folktales, we have the daughter's wish to kill her mother and marry her father transformed through projective inversion into queen (mother) figures dying—with no help from the daughter and therefore no guilt—often with a last request to the king that he marry someone who either looks just like the queen or who can fit into her shoe or ring. The king searches for such a person and comes to realize that it is own daughter who meets these requirements. The father's attempt to marry his daughter (Motif T 411.1 Lecherous father), which occurs in Aarne-Thompson tale type 510B, The Dress of Gold, of Silver, and of Stars, a subtype of Cinderella, would be an example of projective inversion. The daughter's wish to marry her father is transformed into her father's wish to marry her. (Readers who have had contact with small children may well have experienced a small girl's firm statement that she intends to marry Daddy when she grows up.) Again, projective inversion provides an effective means of avoiding guilt. If a father pursues his daughter, then the daughter is surely not to blame.

Having defined projective inversion and attempted to differentiate it from classic or simple projection, we may now turn to the ancient Egyptian tale of two brothers. The fundamental issue is whether or not the tale exemplifies projective inversion, and if it does, can it help us offer a plausible interpretation of the tale's content? The tale consists of two parts. The first part may be identified as the Potiphar's Wife Motif; the second part may be considered a combination of Aarne-Thompson tale type 318, The Faithless Wife, and tale type 590A, The Treacherous Wife. The two portions could also be considered as Proppian moves. (For a fairly technical and detailed Proppian analysis of the tale, see Assmann 1977.) In any event, I hope to show that with the utilization of the concept of projective inversion, the two portions of the tale are deftly integrated and united by a common thematic thread.

If we consider the first portion of the tale, the Potiphar's Wife episode, the crucial question is whether the story concerns an attempt by the wife of Anubis to seduce Bata or is rather a projective inversion of Bata's wish to seduce the wife of his brother. Certainly a literal reading of the "manifest content" of the tale would suggest the first alternative. But can a plausible case be made for the latent content of the tale, that is, the second alternative? Certainly the path of least intellectual resistance would dictate that we be content with just the literal reading. It is not an easy task to advocate any symbolic interpretation of an item of folklore. Freud's own history provides a perfect if controversial analog to this particular question. When several of Freud's patients reported instances of parental molestation to him, he believed them to be factually accurate. Gradually, it dawned on Freud that these alleged parental seductions might be pure fantasy on the part of his patients. It was once again in his important correspondence with Fliess that this dramatic turnabout is documented. In a letter of 21 September 1897, he wrote "I no longer believe in my *neurotica* [theory of the neuroses]" (1985:264). In a letter of 3 January 1899, Freud remarked "a small bit of my self-analysis has forced its way through and confirmed that fantasies are products of later periods and are projected back from what was then the present into earliest childhood . . . To the question "What happened in earliest childhood?" the answer is, "Nothing" (338). Freud's abandonment of the so-called "Seduction Theory" has been the subject of criticism (cf. Masson 1984), but in the present context, one can only applaud Freud's courageous willingness to admit his early error (Bettelheim 1977:320n83). This is not to say that parental molestation never occurs. It certainly does. But that fact does not per se disprove the idea that some patients' reports of seduction attempts by parents can turn out to be fantasied wishful thinking on those patients' part. The relevance of Freud's revolutionary change of heart to the Egyptian tale of two brothers should be obvious. The narrative report of a seduction attempt by a maternal figure might just prove to be a fantasied projective inversion on the part of Bata, the younger brother.

One reason to place credence in the hypothetical projective inversion reading of the tale comes from a basic axiom of fairy tale content. That axiom is: *Fairy tales are always told from a child's perspective.* Fairy tales are never told from the parents' point of view. The hero or heroine, in fact, typically has to defeat usually a same-sex antagonist. Boys have to defeat giants or dragons; girls must defeat wicked stepmothers or witches. These antagonists could be understood as parental imagos. (It is not that parents are literally "giants," but from the ocular perspective of an infant or small child, a parent, using the infant's or child's own measure as a basis of comparison, appears to be a giant.) A corollary of the axiom is that if there are several children in a fairy tale, it is typically the youngest that is the hero or heroine, a clear reflection of inevitable sibling rivalry. What this means is that in the Egyptian tale of two brothers, it is essentially Bata's story, not the story of Anubis's wife, and not the story of Anubis.

The tale makes explicit the fact that the plot includes a reference to mother-son incest. When Anubis's wife propositions Bata, his response is: "Now see, you are like a mother to me. Further, your husband is like a father to me." So this is no idle speculation on the part of a Freudian folklorist. And other scholars have pointed out this overt incestuous aspect (Goldman 1995:34).

Perhaps the most telling detail supporting the idea that the Potiphar's Wife portion of the Egyptian tale of two brothers might be a projective inversion is Bata's self-emasculation. In a 1902 version of the tale from southern Arabia (Horálek 1964a:507, 1968:89) as well as in Dogon and Songai versions in Africa (Paulme 1963:11, 15), it is the elder brother who castrates the younger brother, but in the ancient Egyptian text, the emasculation is definitely self-inflicted. In an unrelated modern Nubian tale recorded in Cairo in 1969, a man attempting to convince his apparently dying wife that he will definitely not remarry obeys her order to emasculate himself (see "The Man Who Severed His Own Thing" in El-Shamy 1999:208–15).

I have already suggested that one of the principal psychological benefits of projective inversions is the avoidance of guilt. In other words, "I didn't try to seduce my mother; she tried to seduce me. It's not my fault." However, the wishful thinker doesn't always get away scot-free. In fairy tales, the hero or heroine is sometimes punished, and sometimes the punishment is self-inflicted! Take the case of Aarne-Thompson tale type 706, The Maiden Without Hands. In this tale, we find a lecherous father who casts his daughter forth when she will not marry him. This is followed by Motif Q 451.1, Hands cut off as punishment. The question is: since it is the father who is ostensibly the villain, why is it that it is the daughter who is punished? The logic of the plot seems somewhat elusive. If, however, we understand the tale in terms of projective inversion, then the logic makes sense. If it is not the father who wants to marry his daughter, but rather the daughter who wants to marry her father, then it is appropriate that it is the daughter who is punished for her incestuous wish. Moreover, if one grants that it could be the daughter's hands that might have been engaged in masturbatory activity (in connection with the fantasied union with her father), then one can appreciate why the punishment involves the maiden's hands. Otto Rank proposed this interpretation of the tale in *Das Inzest-Motif in Dichtung und Sage*, the first edition of which was published in 1912 (1926:367; for a full discussion of the tale, see Dundes 1987).

One can see a parallel between a daughter in flight from her lecherous father who cuts off her masturbatory hands and young Master Bata who cuts off his phallus after being accused of raping his brother's wife (cf. Rank 1926:366). The infliction of physical punishment marks the guilt of both the maiden and Bata. Perhaps the classic example of self-inflicted punishment caused by guilt for an act of mother-son incest is that of Oedipus when he tore out his eyes. Freud and other psychoanalysts interpret the imposition of blindness as the symbolic equivalent of castration (Devereux 1973). In Freud's words, "The blinding in the Oedipus legend and elsewhere is a substitute for castration" (1938:393n1, 907n4). This equation, supported by folkloristic data (Motif J229.12, Prisoners given choice between emasculation and blinding), helps explain why blinding is so common as a punishment for sexual crimes (Devereux 1973:40–42). Just to show how the failure to understand the nature of projective inversion can lead critics astray, I might mention that the conventional wisdom among many Egyptologists is that "Bata's emasculation probably expressed the physical affirmation of his innocence" (Hollis 1990:104). I hope the reader can see the fallacy of this argument. Self-emasculation surely reflects guilt, not innocence!

From a feminist perspective, it is surely significant if it is Bata who is "guilty," for it means that blaming Potiphar's wife for what is essentially a male "crime" is yet another example of men cleverly casting women as the villain. The episode, read literally, without the benefit of an understanding of projective inversion, makes Potiphar's wife just one more in an endless series of women depicted as evil, beguiling, seductive creatures, a classic case of blaming the victim.

In the Potiphar's Wife episode in the Old Testament, there is no evidence of emasculation. But I would argue that in all versions of the Potiphar's Wife plot, it is a matter of projective inversion and that it is the son who is "guilty" of an Oedipal incestuous wish. Interestingly enough, there are several post-biblical commentaries, including the Babylonian Talmud, that suggested that Joseph was guilty of desiring Potiphar's wife (Kugel 1990:94; Goldman 1995:37, Levinson 1997:274). In the account in Genesis, it is not Joseph's phallus that is ripped off, but his garment: "And she caught him by his garment, saying, Lie with me: and he left his garment in her hand" (Genesis 39:12), a detail reminiscent of Joseph's brothers stripping Joseph of his coat of many colors (Genesis 37:23). In the version of the Potiphar's wife episode found in the Koran, an unnamed woman member of the wife's entourage proposes an ingenious test to determine who is telling the truth. Incidentally, the fact that this woman is not named is parallel to Potiphar's wife not being named, which in turn is part of the same larger pattern that denies names to Mrs. Noah, Mrs. Lot, and Mrs. Job, among others, a definite patriarchal bias against women (cf. Goldman 1995:85). The test (Sura 12:26) consisted of ascertaining whether Joseph's garment was ripped from the front or the back. Since the garment was torn from behind, this confirmed Joseph's account of fleeing from the would-be seductress.

A more likely allusion to emasculation in the Old Testament account, according to some Biblical commentaries, is the hint that Potiphar may have been a eunuch, incapable of having sexual relations with his wife (Kugel 1990:75, Goldman 1995:84, Péter-Contesse 1996). In any case, from the perspective of Oedipal psychology, it is of some significance that according to the Babylonian Talmud, Joseph checks his erotic impulse when "the image of his *father* entered and appeared to him in the window" (Kugel 1990:95, my emphasis, Levinson 1997:278).

The theme of castration (in the sense of emasculation, not just the removal of testicles) is found in both portions of the tale. The crocodiles in the river that separate Bata and Anubis could be construed as a kind of riverine castratory threat (Motif F 547.1.1, Vagina Dentata). Hollis is correct in saying that Anubis could not get at his younger brother Bata "because of the crocodiles" (Hollis 1990:9), but what she does not say is that the jaws of these creatures constituted a threat to Anubis of castration. The placement of the heart on the top of a pine tree is yet another signal of emasculation when one realizes that in ancient Egyptian folk belief, "the semen of the male, by which the woman was impregnated, emanated from the heart" (125, for an extended discussion of the "penis-heart" motif that ends with a consideration of the tale of two brothers, see Slater 1968:265–76). In the second portion of the tale, the castration theme is repeated. The tree where Bata's semen-producing heart was placed is cut down, which kills Bata. The bull transform of Bata is slaughtered, but two drops of bull's blood produce two trees. (It is curious that Joseph in the Old Testament is also described as a bull with strong horns [Deuteronomy 33:17].) The two trees are also cut down, but "a splinter flew and entered the mouth of the noblewoman." In each instance, Bata miraculously survives the castration attacks by the pharaoh.

Perhaps the most amazing feat of all is Bata's impregnating his former wife so as to be reborn from her. This act would also seem to defy logic. But by being a self-begetter, a son becomes one with his father. Fulfilling an Oedipal ideal, he thereby assumes a procreative role with his father's wife. But since the pharaoh/father's wife was originally *his* wife, we have another example of projective inversion. The son would like his mother to be his wife, but this is a taboo thought involving incest. So in the projective inversion, it is Bata the son's original wife who becomes his mother.

One might wonder if anyone has previously probed the possible psychological significance of the Egyptian tale of two brothers. The answer is affirmative. In 1913, Otto Rank teamed up with fellow psychoanalyst Hanns Sachs to write *Die Bedeutung der Psychoanalyse für die Geisteswissenschaften*. The second chapter was concerned with "The Investigation of Myths and Legends" (1964:33–72) and was almost certainly written entirely by Rank, whose expertise in folklore among the early psychoanalysts was unmatched. In that chapter, Rank presents an analysis of the Egyptian tale of two brothers. His comments include: "Thus Bata strives from the beginning to seduce the 'mother,' whom he, in the second part ever pursues in symbolic disguise, which plainly betrays that the slander by her at the beginning of the narrative is to be considered only as a projection of his incestuous wish" (60). His concluding summary: "Thus the hero of the Egyptian brother legend, who wishes to seduce the mother, is driven out by the favored rival (father, brother) (pursuit with drawn knife) or castrated (self-castration) or killed (abode in the cedar valley). The picture of the mother, however, follows him everywhere; he lives with the god-wife until she is taken from him by the king, in whom we recognize a father image. The hero follows her to the court, which represents nothing else than the wished-for return to the parental home (rendered unrecognizable), where the son can carry out in a cover picture of strange persons, the unallowed wish gratifications denied by reality" (70).

A second psychoanalytic interpretation of the tale of two brothers was proposed by Bruno Bettelheim in *The Uses of Enchantment*. Bettelheim, however, seems unsure whether the primary projection is the wife's or Bata's. "This ancient Egyptian tale contains the elements of a person accused of what the accuser himself wants to do: the wife accuses the younger brother, whom she tried to seduce, of seducing her. Thus, the plot describes the projection of an unacceptable tendency in oneself onto another person; this suggests that such projections are as ancient as man. Since the story is told from the brothers' side, it's also possible that the younger brother projected his desires onto his older brother's wife, accusing her of what he wanted to but dared not do" (1977:92) Bettelheim, incidentally, does not refer to Rank's earlier more detailed interpretation of the tale, although elsewhere he does mention Rank's *Psychoanalytische Beiträge zur Mythenforschung* (313n11), which reprinted his analysis of the two brothers (Rank 1922:130–37, 143). On the other hand, Bettelheim had a bad habit of borrowing ideas from other authors without proper acknowledgement (Dundes 1991).

Another psychoanalytic interpretation of the tale, not cited by Bettelheim (or Hollis), was offered by Philip Slater in his brilliant book *The Glory of Hera* (1968:276–82). Slater sees Bata as "an oedipal hero" in a tale involving projection in that "Instead of taking his mother-wife away from the Pharaoh, his father the Pharaoh takes her away from him. Similarly projective is the Potiphar's-wife theme, in which oedipal guilt is projected onto the woman. This is not entirely successful, however, for subsequent events reveal traces of Bata's own guilt. It is difficult to see, for example, why he feels called upon to castrate himself and go into exile if he is not in fact guilty" (279). Except for substituting "projective inversion" for "projection," I could not possibly improve upon Slater's analysis.

Folklorists with their typical antipathy to psychoanalytic theory have totally ignored the interpretations offered by Rank, Bettelheim, and Slater. At least Egyptologist Hollis, to her credit, did, in her thorough dissertation devoted to the tale of two brothers, cite Rank and Bettelheim in her brief survey of "Psychological Approaches" (1990:37–40). However, Hollis dismisses these interpretations, suggesting that such interpreters err in forcing the material to conform to modern psychological theories. In her condescending words, "It is certainly inappropriate to call these approaches wrong, but it cannot be said they really elucidate the tale's meaning for its own time" (40). In her paper on the Potiphar's Wife motif, Hollis needs only one sentence to rule out any psychoanalytic considerations: "A psychoanalytic approach also could be taken, but the speculativeness of such an analysis would add little to this discussion" (1989:31). Hollis's own predilection is for a myth-ritual interpretation, the clear-cut favorite theory of Egyptologists and other Middle East scholars. So committed are such scholars to myth-ritual theory that an alleged ritual origin is inevitably postulated even when there is no actual empirical evidence that such a ritual ever existed. Egyptologist Assmann, for instance, assumes an initiation ritual underlies the tale (1977:23–24) even though, as Hollis points out, no Egyptian initiation rite can be related to this story (1990:46, 165). Hollis adopts what she considers to be a more modest myth-ritual position. "There is clearly no question that the tale presents a rite of passage" (165) even though, once again, precious little ethnographic data supporting such a "ritual" origin can be adduced. Hollis is equally convinced that the same pattern applies to the Potiphar's Wife episode in Genesis: "It is important to observe that in its overall presentation, the Potiphar's wife episode constitutes the first part of a rite of passage according to the classic tripartite formulation of Arnold van Gennep" (1989:32). One can only marvel at the logic that precludes a psychoanalytic approach on the grounds that it involves "speculativeness," while at the same time advocating a myth-ritual approach that postulates the existence of a totally hypothetical "rite of passage," which is assumed to underlie the Potiphar's Wife motif in the Old Testament.

We conclude on the basis of the above analysis that the two portions of the Egyptian tale of two brothers seem to reflect similar psychological themes, and that, in my opinion, is why the tale seems to be so well integrated and coherent. And it is precisely those themes that should be of interest to modern readers. The ancient Egyptian tale of two brothers is more than simply proof of the continuity of the content of *märchen*, as Finnish folklorist Kaarle Krohn observed (1931:283). The tale also confirms the existence of the psychological device of projective inversion over a period of three thousand years. That provides an important piece of evidence against the tired and specious Freud-bashing argument that psychoanalytic theory, if it is valid at all, applies only to Jews living in *fin de siècle* Vienna. Moreover, its validity would argue against Hollis's rather peremptory dismissive comment that such an interpretation cannot elucidate the tale's meaning for its own time. If classical Greece presents dramatic evidence of the existence of Oedipal psychology, there is no reason that classical Egypt cannot have done likewise. Psychological theories may well be modern, but human psychology is surely as ancient as humans themselves, and folklorists should exult in the fact that such human psychology is so artfully displayed in folktales.

References Cited

Aarne, Antti. 1910. *Verzeichnis der Märchentypen*. Helsinki: Academia Scientiarum Fennica.
Aarne, Antti, and Stith Thompson. 1961. *The Types of the Folktale*. 2nd rev. FF Communications No. 184. Helsinki: Academia Scientiarum Fennica.
Assmann, Jan. 1977. Das ägyptische Zweibrüdermärchen (Papyrus D'Orbiney. *Zeitschrift für Ägyptische Sprache und Altertumskunde* 104:1–25.
Aycock, Alan. 1992. Potiphar's Wife: Prelude to a Structural Analysis. *Man* 27:479–94.
Bellak, Leopold. 1944. The Concept of Projection. *Psychiatry* 7:353–70.
Bettelheim, Bruno. 1977. *The Uses of Enchantment*. New York: Vintage.
Blankenburg, Wolfgang. 1975. Voraussetzungen der Projektionstheorie. *Confinia Psychiatrica* 18:207–20.
Bloomfield, Maurice. 1923. Joseph and Potiphar in Hindu Fiction. *Transactions of the American Philological Association* 54:141–67.
Cosquin, E. 1877. Un Problème historique à propos du conte égyptien des deux frères. *Revue des Questions Historiques* 22:502–16.
Devereux, George. 1973. The Self-Blinding of Oidipous in Sophokles' *Oidipous Tyrannos*. *Journal of Hellenic Studies* 93:36–49.
Dundes, Alan. 1980. *Interpreting Folklore*. Bloomington: Indiana University Press.
———. 1987. The Psychoanalytic Study of the Grimms' Tales With Special Reference to 'The Maiden Without Hands' (AT 706). *Germanic Review* 62:50–65.
———. 1991. Bruno Bettelheim's Uses of Enchantment and Abuses of Scholarship. *Journal of American Folklore* 104:74–83.
Edmunds, Lowell. 1985. *Oedipus: The Ancient Legend and Its Later Analogues*. Baltimore: Johns Hopkins University Press.
El-Shamy, Hasan M. 1995. *Folk Traditions of the Arab World: A Guide to Motif Classification*. 2 vols. Bloomington: Indiana University Press.
———. 1999. *Tales Arab Women Tell and the Behavioral Patterns They Portray*. Bloomington: Indiana University Press.
Faverty, Frederic Everett. 1931. The Story of Joseph and Potiphar's Wife in Mediaeval Literature. *Harvard Studies and Notes in Philology and Literature* 13:81–127.
Freud, Sigmund. 1938. *The Basic Writings of Sigmund Freud*. New York: Random House.
———. 1959. *Collected Papers*. 5 vols. New York: Basic Books.
———. 1985. *The Complete Letters of Sigmund Freud to Wilhelm Fliess. 1887–1904*. Trans. and ed. Jeffrey Moussaieff Masson. Cambridge: Harvard University Press.
Geertz, Clifford. 1968. Ethos, World-View and the Analysis of Sacred Symbols. In *Every Man His Way*. Ed. Alan Dundes. 301–15. Englewood Cliffs, N.J.: Prentice-Hall.

Goldman, Shalom. 1995. *The Wiles of Women/The Wiles of Men: Joseph and Potiphar's Wife in Ancient Near Eastern, Jewish, and Islamic Folklore.* Albany: State University of New York Press.

Grey, Leslie. 1990. *A Concordance of Buddhist Birth Stories.* Oxford: Pali Text Society.

———. 1998. Supplement to *The Concordance of the Buddhist Birth Stories. Journal of the Pali Text Society* 24:103–47.

Hollis, Susan Tower. 1989. The Woman in Ancient Examples of the Potiphar's Wife Motif, K2111. In *Gender and Difference in Ancient Israel.* Ed. Peggy L. Day. 28–42. Minneapolis: Fortress Press.

———. 1990. *The Ancient Egyptian "Tale of Two Brothers": The Oldest Fairy Tale in the World.* Norman: University of Oklahoma Press.

———. 1995. Tales of Magic and Wonder from Ancient Egypt. In *Civilizations of the Ancient Near East.* Ed. Jack M. Sasson. 2255–64. 4 vols. New York: Simon and Schuster Macmillan.

Horálek, Karel. 1964a. Ein Beitrag zu dem Studium der Afrikanischen Märchen. *Archiv Orientální* 32:501–21.

———. 1964b. Ein Beitrag zur volkskundlichen Balkanologie. *Fabula* 7:1–32.

———. 1968. Le conte des deux frères (Anoubis et Bata): Un coup d'oeil retrospectif et la revue des variantes orientales. In *Man and Culture* II: Contributions of the Czechoslovak Ethnologists for the VIII International Congress of Anthropological and Ethnological Sciences in Tokyo. 80–98. Prague: Czechoslovak Academy of Sciences.

———. 1978a. The Balkan Variants of *Anup and Bata*: AT 315B. In *Studies in East European Narrative,* ed. Linda Dégh. 231–62. Bloomington: Indiana University Folklore Institute.

———. 1978b. Brüdermärchen: Das ägyptische Brüder. *Enzyklopädie des Märchens* 2:925–40.

Jason, Heda, and Aharon Kempinski. 1981. How Old Are Folktales? *Fabula* 22:1–27.

Krohn, Kaarle. 1931. Zum neugefundenen ägyptischen Märchen. *Zeitschrift für Volkskunde* 41:281–83.

Kugel, James L. 1990. *In Potiphar's House.* San Francisco: HarperCollins.

Lang, Andrew. 1899. *Myth, Ritual and Religion.* 2 vols. London: Longmans, Green, and Co.

Levinson, Joshua. 1997. An-Other Woman: Joseph and Potiphar's Wife. Staging the Body Politic. *Jewish Quarterly Review* 87:269–301.

Lindzey, Gardner. 1961. *Projective Techniques and Cross-Cultural Research.* New York: Appleton-Century-Crofts.

Mannhardt, W. 1859. Das älteste Märchen: Satu und Anepu oder die beiden brüder. *Zeitschrift für deutsche Mythologie und Sittenkunde* 4:232–59.

Masson, Jeffrey Moussaieff. 1984. *The Assault on Truth: Freud's Suppression of the Seduction Theory.* New York: Farrar, Straus and Giroux.

Mat'e, M. E. 1964. The Myth and Folktale of Ancient Egypt as a Source for Studying the History of the Family. *Soviet Anthropology and Archeology* 3(2):35–42.

Paulme, Denise. 1963. Un conte de fées africain: le garçon travesti ou Joseph en Afrique. *L'Homme* 3(2):7–21.

Penzer, N. M. ed. 1924–28. *The Ocean of Story.* 10 vols. London: Chas. J. Sawyer.

Péter-Contesse, René. 1996. Was Potiphar a Eunuch? (Genesis 37.36; 39.1). *Bible Translator* 47:142–46.

Rank, Otto. 1922. *Psychoanalytische Beiträge zur Mythenforschung.* 2nd ed. Leipzig: Internationale psychoanalytische Bibliothek.

———. 1926. *Das Inzest-Motiv in Dichtung und Sage.* 2nd ed. Leipzig: Franz Deuticke.

———. 1959. *The Myth of the Birth of the Hero.* New York: Vintage.

Rank, Otto, and Hanns Sachs. 1964. The Significance of Psychoanalysis for the Humanities. *American Imago* 21:6–133.

Rooth, Anna Birgitta. 1951. *The Cinderella Cycle.* Lund: Gleerup.

Rycroft, Charles. 1968. *A Critical Dictionary of Psycho-Analysis.* New York: Basic Books.

Slater, Philip. 1968. *The Glory of Hera: Greek Mythology and the Greek Family.* Boston: Beacon Press.

Thompson, Stith. 1946. *The Folktale.* New York: Dryden Press.

———. 1955–58. *Motif-Index of Folk-Literature.* 6 vols. Bloomington: Indiana University Press.

Von Sydow, C. W. 1930. Den fornegyptiska sagan om de tva bröderna. *Vetenskapssocietetens i Lund Arsbok* 53–89.

———. 1948. *Selected Papers on Folklore.* Copenhagen: Rosenkilde and Bagger.

Vries, Jan de. 1954. *Betrachtungen zum Märchen.* FF Communications No. 150. Helsinki: Academia Scientiarum Fennica.

Yohannan, John D. 1968. *Joseph and Potiphar's Wife in World Literature.* New York: New Directions.

4

The Trident and the Fork

DISNEY'S "THE LITTLE MERMAID" AS A MALE CONSTRUCTION OF AN ELECTRAL FANTASY

(with Lauren Dundes)

Most of the tales written by Hans Christian Andersen were not taken from oral tradition. Although he occasionally borrowed motifs from such tradition, the greater portion of his so-called fairy tales were strictly literary creations. The distinguished Danish folklorist Bengt Holbek claimed that of some 156 "fairy tales and stories" published by Andersen, "only seven of them are manifestly taken from Danish oral tradition" (Holbek, 1990, p. 165), a number confirmed by Grönbech (1996, p. 221). On the other hand, Elias Bredsdorff in his splendid biography of Andersen suggests that "nine tales were based on folktales Andersen had heard" (1975, p. 311). Whether the number is seven or nine, there can be no question that the percentage of authentic traditional tales in Andersen's total corpus is small.

In the parlance of folkloristics, the academic study of folklore, such literary creations are usually referred to as "Kunstmärchen" as opposed to "Volksmärchen." There is a huge body of such literary or art tales, many of which have become a staple in the canon of children's literature. One of Andersen's literary tales that has received such hallowed status is his classic "The Little Mermaid" (1837). In one of his letters, Andersen acknowledged proudly that whereas his first tales were "mostly old ones" he had "heard as a child," the later ones that were his "own creations such as 'The Little Mermaid' . . . were the most popular" (Bredsdorff, 1975, p. 165).

56   "The Little Mermaid" as Male Construction of Electral Fantasy

In "The Little Mermaid," Andersen utilizes two major folklore motifs. The first is the very figure of the mermaid, a young girl whose lower parts consist of a substantial fish's tail. The figure is listed in the six-volume *Motif-Index of Folk-Literature* as "Motif B81. *Mermaid.* Woman with tail of fish. Lives in sea." The mermaid is not universal—no motif, for that matter, is universal in the sense of existing among all peoples past and present. It is not found in native North and South America, for example. There are many accounts of female supernatural creatures inhabiting watery domains (Moog, 1987; Róheim, 1948), but most of them do not refer to demonic beings with fish-like lower extremities. Although not universal, the mermaid or some early form thereof is well attested in classical antiquity (Deonna, 1928; Faral, 1953; Shepard, 1940) and is significantly represented in ancient, medieval (Almendral Oppermann, 1992; Broendsted, 1965; Goodman, 1983; Leclercq-Marx, 1997) and modern (Liberati, 1995) art.

There is some confusion of the mermaid figure with the siren (Marót, 1958; Rachewiltz, 1987) and apparently the evolution of the mermaid from the siren involved a shift from ornithomorphic to pisciform features. Just when the siren lost her bird-like appearance and obtained her fish-tail to become the "modern" mermaid is in dispute (Benwell and Waugh, 1961, p. 48; Burnel, 1949, p. 201). One authority claims that the earliest mention of a fish-tailed siren occurred around the turn of the 8th century (Phillpotts, 1980, p. 32), while another indicates the 6th century (Touchefeu-Meynier, 1962, p. 450). There have been numerous alleged sightings of mermaids (Waugh, 1960) as well as repeated attempts to display fake mermaid specimens in circus freak shows (Bondeson, 1999, pp. 36–63). Though few now believe in the existence of actual mermaids—one scientific parody deplores the absence of mermaid skeletons, which might have been used as an index of mermaid population statistics (Banse, 1990, p. 151)—the popularity of the mermaid figure continues unabated in modern literature (Roebling, 1991), movies (Bouillet, 1958), as well as in jokes and cartoons (Johnson, 1987).

The second motif as identified in the standard international *Motif-Index of Folk-Literature* mentioned above is K1911. *The false bride (substituted bride).* An impostor takes the wife's place without the husband's knowledge. This second motif, though critical for an understanding of the plot of "The Little Mermaid" has not received much attention by

"The Little Mermaid" as Male Construction of Electral Fantasy 57

students of either Andersen's 1837 story or Disney's 1989 feature-length cartoon adaptation. In Andersen's narrative, the mermaid saves the prince from drowning in a shipwreck caused by a storm. But later having forfeited her voice (by having her tongue cut out) to the sea witch in exchange for having her fish tail replaced by human legs, she is unable to reveal her identity to the prince. The prince mistakenly believes the princess of a neighboring kingdom was the one who had saved him. In the Disney version, it is Ursula, the sea witch, who transforms herself into a beautiful young woman and who, armed with the mermaid Ariel's exquisite voice, persuades Prince Eric that it was she who saved him thereby causing him to seek to marry her. (The seductive power of Ariel's singing voice is an echo of the original siren figure.) As we shall see, the failure to take account of the false or substituted bride motif has greatly impeded the analysis of the underlying symbolic content of Disney's "The Little Mermaid."

The various interpretative essays devoted to the Disney film include structural (Thomsen, 1990), moralistic (Hastings, 1993), feminist (O'Brien, 1996; Trites, 1990–1991), and psychoanalytic (Soracco, 1990; Tseëlon, 1995) approaches among others (Nybo, 1990). Folkloristic treatments (Bendix, 1993; Ingwersen and Ingwersen, 1990) emphasize Disney's utilization of folktale formulas, e.g. the traditional happy ending. Not all discussions of Disney's transformation of Andersen's plot are equally sophisticated. Tseëlon, for instance, argues that the Disney version has changed the character of the story by turning "the myth into a folktale" (1995, p. 1026). Calling Andersen's story a "myth" reveals a serious error in genre identification. A myth, defined in concrete technical terms, is a traditional sacred narrative explaining how the earth and humankind came to be in their present form. Andersen's "The Little Mermaid" is not a traditional narrative; it is mostly a literary product of his creative imagination. It is not sacred as it does not explain how the earth and humankind came to be in their present form. Tseëlon's claim that it is a myth is based upon her mistaken notion that "a myth is a story which involves supernatural beings" (1995, p. 1018), but the vast majority of stories involving supernatural beings (such as fairies, ghosts, vampires—and mermaids) are legends. A legend is a narrative told as true and set in the post-creation world. Andersen's "The Little Mermaid" would thus be more correctly classified as a "literary legend."

It is true that the Disney transform of Andersen's literary legend has elements of a folktale, but it would be more accurate to specify the particular kind of folktale. Folktales are fictional narratives and they include animal tales, cumulative and other formula tales, and jokes. The particular form of folktale relevant to the Disney film is the so-called magic and wonder tale (misleadingly labeled in English as "fairy tale"). In the standard canonical index of Indo-European folktales, tales of magic or fairy tales are limited to Aarne-Thompson tale types 300–749 (Aarne and Thompson, 1961, pp. 88–254). There are very few fairies found in fairy tales and most accounts of fairies are told as true and would accordingly therefore be more appropriately classified as legends, not folktales. One of the characteristics of fairy tales is that they typically end with a marriage as the Russian folklorist Vladimir Propp so brilliantly demonstrated in his pathbreaking *Morphology of the Folktale*, first published in 1928. The final function of the sequence of 31 functions or units of plot action identified by Propp in his corpus of 100 Russian fairy tales is labeled "Wedding" (1968, p. 63).

In Andersen's original story, the little mermaid does not marry the handsome prince and this sad story of unrequited or unfulfilled heterosexual love has been linked to Andersen's own personal life (Bredsdorff, 1975, pp. 280–282, 348; Golden, 1998, p. 100; Griffith, 1984; Lederer, 1986, pp. 169–172) and what appear in retrospect to be his latent homosexual tendencies. As a small boy, Andersen played with dolls even to the extent of sewing dresses for them; as a youth he studied briefly at the Royal Ballet in Copenhagen in an abortive attempt to become a ballet dancer; one of his principal life-long hobbies was making amusing paper cut-outs; never married, he appears to have had a long-standing "crush" on his patron Jonas Collin's son Edvard to whom he wrote many "love" letters; and as an old man, he invariably invited one of Jonas Collin's young grandsons to accompany him on his many travels abroad (Bredsdorff, 1975, p. 19, 22, 85, 303). The question of whether or not Andersen was a repressed homosexual remains moot, but it has been the subject of much debate (Hansen, 1901; Helweg, 1927, 1929; Lederer, 1986; Ringblom, 1997; von Rosen, 1978–1981, Bech, 1998). Certainly, Andersen seems to have identified with his mermaid creation. As one critic phrased it, Andersen "is the little mermaid, the outsider who came from the depths and was never really accepted in the new world into which he moved" and Andersen himself confessed that the story was one of only two of all his works that moved him deeply while writing it (Bredsdorff, 1975, pp. 275, 125).

In any case, Andersen is given credit or rather blame for transforming the traditional seductive, aggressive mermaid figure into a passive self-effacing heroine who sacrifices her own goals and fulfillment for the sake of the happiness of an unattainable male prince (Golden, 1998, p. 99; Stuby, 1992, p. 109). A female psychiatrist begins her book entitled *Sweet Suffering: Woman as Victim* with a report of one of her patient's first analytic sessions in which the patient recounted the story of Andersen's "The Little Mermaid." The psychiatrist comments: "This story is a nearly perfect parable of masochism, for it expresses the self-punishment, the submission to another, and the sense of suffering that lie at the heart of masochistic behavior" (Shainess, 1984, pp. 1–2). It is perfectly true that the pre-Andersen mermaid was a very different creature, a dangerously seductive combination of voluptuousness and voracity. One description may stand for many. In 1601, a Portuguese priest living in Brazil wrote the following vivid account of "Mermen, or men of the Sea":

> The female are like women, they have long haire and are beautiful . . . In Port Secure are some seene, which have killed some Indians alreadie, the manner of their killing is to embrace themselves with the person, so strongly, kissing, and grasping it hard to it selfe, that they crush it in pieces remaining whole, and when they perceive it dead, they give some sighings in shew of sorrow, and letting them goe they runne away, and if they carrie any they eate only the eies, the nose, the points of the fingers and toes, and privie members, and so ordinarily they are found on the sands with these things missing. (Tristaon 1601, p. 1315)

In Disney's adaptation of Andersen's story of a passive mermaid, the addition of the final wedding scene has further incurred the wrath of feminists who see it as an insidious continuation of a patriarchal conspiracy to keep women enslaved. The Little Mermaid is initially controlled by her father Triton, the king of the sea, who eventually hands her over to her husband Prince Eric. Never really free, Ariel is allowed only to transfer her allegiance and abode from one male to another. (The patronymic tradition in Western culture supports this metaphorically as a woman is expected to exchange her original father's last name for that of her husband. Also American wedding ritual typically requires the father—not the mother—to escort his daughter-bride down the church aisle to formally give her away to the groom.) Moreover, the fact that Ariel is unable to speak means that she is quite literally "dumb." Feminists feel, with some justification, that this further confirms the male chauvinist ideal of a woman who is beautiful but dumb, in this case not just unintelligent, but mute (Golden, 1998, p. 140; Tseëlon, 1995, p. 1022).

Feminists further complain, again with good reason, that Disney has continued the tradition begun by Andersen by making the alleged "heroine" of his film a very passive creature who relies on the assistance of a number of animal allies, all of whom are male. She does not kill the evil sea witch Ursula (the only powerful female portrayed); Prince Eric does so (cf. O'Brien, 1996, p. 173; Trites, 1990–1991, pp. 150–151). She can remain human and marry Eric, not by kissing him, but by inducing *him* to kiss *her*. Even in Andersen's story, the mermaid in search of a soul can obtain one only if the prince allows his soul to "flow" into her body—the receiving body aperture is not indicated in this sublimated image of coitus (Dahlerup, 1990, p. 420). In contrast, in true oral fairy tales, the heroine is the active agent. So in Hansel and Gretel (the very naming of this tale reflects a male bias . . . It is Gretel's story, not Hansel's), Gretel kills the witch, a double of her mother who was the original instigator of the plot to dispose of the children by abandoning them in the woods. (It was only after the fourth edition of the *Kinder- und Hausmärchen* that the Grimm brothers changed the figure of the mother to "stepmother" no doubt in an effort to avoid further besmirching the image of motherhood in traditional German culture.) When men retell women's tales, the tales are often altered to conform to male ideology. So in the oral versions of Little Red Riding Hood, the heroine escapes from the wolf (or tigress in the Chinese, Japanese, and Korean versions) by her own cleverness and ingenuity. This is not the case in the male retellings of the tale. In the Perrault version, she is eaten up by the wolf and also in the Grimm version, where unable to rescue herself, she must await a passing male huntsman to save her (cf. Zipes, 1993, pp. 29, 79). In this context, it is not totally unexpected that the Disney version of "The Little Mermaid" continues the passive female tradition, even if this is clearly disappointing to feminist critics. On the other hand, Ariel does defy her controlling father by visiting humans and in her unrelenting single-minded quest to win the love of Prince Eric.

What is most striking about the Disney adaptation of Andersen's "The Little Mermaid" is the remarkable series of symbolic representations of a young girl's coming of age and her successful, if conventional, resolution of the Electra Complex. Several studies of the Andersen story have concentrated on the process of individuation (Engel, 1988; Mäeenpää-Reenkola, 1989; for another Jungian study of the story, see Nyborg, 1962, pp. 68–8 and the polemic dialogue it generated: Baggesen, 1967a, b; Nyborg, 1967). It was actually Jung who first proposed the term "Electra Complex" for the female counterpart of the Oedipus Complex in a series of lectures on psychoanalysis that he presented at the Fordham University medical school in September 1912. Speaking about the Oedipus Complex, he said, "The conflict takes on a more masculine and therefore more typical form in a son, whereas a daughter develops a specific liking for the father, with a corresponding jealous attitude towards the mother. We could call this the Electra complex" (Jung, 1975, p. 72). The fact that it was Jung who coined the term may explain in part why Freud opposed its adoption, preferring instead to employ the label "Oedipus complex" for both son–mother and daughter–father constellations: "I do not see any advance or gain in the introduction of the term 'Electra complex', and do not advocate its use" (1920, p. 155, n. 1). On the other hand, from a feminist perspective, it seems inappropriate to use a male-centered folktale—Oedipus is tale type 931 in the standard index of European folktales; see Aarne and Stith Thompson, 1961—to describe a female psychological configuration. However, Freud's succinct description of the complex in his lecture on "Femininity" in his 1932 *New Introductory Lectures on Psycho-Analysis* would certainly seem to be applicable to Disney's "The Little Mermaid": ". . . in the Oedipus situation the girl's father has become her love-object, and we expect that in the normal course of development she will find her way from this paternal object to her final choice of an object" (1932, pp. 118–119). Ariel must shift from loving her father to loving her husband-to-be Eric.

Ariel's mermaid image itself contains a basic paradox. As a young girl, she is quite literally divided. Her lower "human" half is denied. This division is paralleled by the dichotomy between the lower world, under the sea, and the upper world where human libido is permitted to function.

Ariel's father, King Triton, assumes she will marry a merman who, like other merfolk, lacks genitals, whereby permanent virginity may be guaranteed. (It remains a mystery as to exactly how mer-people manage to reproduce.) As Dorothy Dinnerstein correctly observed in writing in 1967 about Andersen's story, the mermaid's renunciation of her tail for human legs "means sudden human-sexual availability" (1967, p. 106). (It is interesting in this connection that inasmuch as fish are apodal, it is their caudal fin or their "tail" which replaces the normal female lower limbs in mermaid anatomy. Ariel must lose her "tail" to become human.) On the other hand, the mermaid has to pay a price for gaining human sexual parts. Through a curious form of upward displacement, she is obliged to let the sea witch cut out her tongue. In other words, she is forced to give up her upper part in order to have her lower part. In the Disney version, this is softened so that she loses only her voice. The voice, however, is also a sexual component as it is what attracts Eric in the first place. Dinnerstein interprets the tongueless mouth as the male perception of the woman as a mutilated (castrated?) male. She terms it a horrible wound, a nightmare vagina, "an empty hole created by excision" (1967, p. 108). Other critics also see the cutting out of the mermaid's tongue as a form of castration (Consoli, 1974, p. 87, 1980, p. 80; Duve, 1967, p. 141; Johansen, 1996, pp. 219–220; Soracco, 1990, p. 408; Tseëlon, 1995, p. 1023). This castratory incident should, however, be viewed in the total context of the tale where it can be seen as part of the larger struggle between males and females as to who shall finally possess power as symbolized by a phallus.

The idea that a mermaid is to be destroyed or transformed is signaled early in the Disney film. Eric's ship has on the cutwater of its prow a mermaid figurehead. When he explains to his counselor Grimsby that he expects to fall in love one day as if struck by lightning, through the magic of his words and the "omnipotence of thought", lightning suddenly strikes the ship and the mermaid figurehead is roughly dislodged from its privileged position on the bow. The resulting jagged edge of the ship will play an important role in the denouement of the plot later on.

Also early in the film, Ariel is seen exploring the interior of a sunken ship where she is searching for human artifacts to add to her collection of such objects which she stores in a secret place. Remembering that ships are commonly regarded as female (and referred to by means of fe-

"The Little Mermaid" as Male Construction of Electral Fantasy 63

male pronouns), it is of symbolic significance that she is investigating the interior of a ship. While rummaging about, Ariel is suddenly threatened by a hostile shark. She is saved only when the shark in an attempt to attack her (and her animal companion) gets his head caught in the upper ring portion of an anchor. (The ring with its descending shank and horizontal stock clearly suggest the standard symbol for a female, commonly referred to as Venus' hand mirror.) The phallic shark is thus rendered harmless and impotent by being tightly wedged in a female enclosure.

In the ship, Ariel does discover several objects, one of which is a fork. She does not know what it is for and when she subsequently asks a friendly but befuddled seagull about it, he informs her that it is a kind of comb. Later on land while at dinner with Prince Eric, Ariel makes a fool of herself by attempting to comb her hair at the table using a fork. The fork may be contrasted with the trident possessed by her father Triton, the king of the sea. The trident is also a kind of fork but it is much larger and endowed with magical power. Both Ariel's fork and Triton's trident are trifurcated (whereas the dinner fork of Prince Eric's advisor Grimsby has four tines). The fork is significant in terms of both its form and its size. Its form includes tines located at its bottom. Tines may perhaps suggest the bifurcation of the mermaid's tail into human legs. Ariel must learn to use a fork properly just as she must learn to walk on two legs. Her placing of the fork in her hair could allude to her grappling with her newly found sexual parts (which include pubic hair) created by the bifurcation. The seagull advising Ariel had mistakenly informed her that the fork was a "dingle-hopper," a curious seemingly nonsensical word which may or may not allude to the slang term "dingle" meaning penis (Spears, 1990, p. 51) wherein the sexual implications of learning to handle a "penis" hopper, that is, someone who hops on a penis, would be obvious.

The size of the fork (when compared to the trident) emphasizes the differential proportions of adult and child. Both Triton and the villainous sea witch Ursula are huge figures whereas Ariel is small. The adjectival prefix "Little" placed before "Mermaid" serves to infantilize Ariel. This is similar to the same device in the name of "Little" Red Riding Hood. (In French, it is Le <u>Petit</u> Chaperon Rouge and in German the suffix <u>-chen</u> signifying diminutive in Rotkäppchen accomplishes the same result.) Of course, if we remember that fairy tales are always told from the child's perspective, then giants are nothing more than the child's perception of adults. Relativistically speaking, the child does not see him or herself as small but rather adults are perceived as larger versions of the observing child.

Ariel's initial family situation is revealing. Her mother is absent (Leadbeater and Wilson, 1993, p. 472) and we are told nothing about her. King Triton lives with his six daughters of which Ariel is the youngest and obviously his favorite. In female-centered fairy tales, the mother is often absent or killed thereby leaving the father and daughter alone. This is parallel to male-centered fairy tales, where it is the father who is absent. An example would be "Jack and the Beanstalk" where Jack lives alone with his mother. Following adventures in which Jack successfully hides in the giant's wife's oven, he kills the giant by cutting down a huge stalk with an ax handed to him by his mother with whom he ends up living happily ever after (Róheim, 1953, pp. 358–359). As male-centered fairy tales present Oedipal plots where sons castrate or kill fathers, so female-centered fairy tales present Electral plots where daughters triumph over mothers or mother surrogates such as witches or wicked stepmothers.

In Disney's "The Little Mermaid," the mother substitute to be defeated is clearly Ursula, the sea witch (Leadbeater and Wilson, 1993, pp. 477, 478). When Ariel feels thwarted by her father in her quest to pursue Prince Eric, she goes behind her father's back, turning to the mother substitute for assistance, just as children often turn to the other parent when the first one refuses to help. In the Electra Complex, the daughter competes with her mother for the attention (love) of her father. According to Freud's Oedipal theory, a girl wants to marry her father or a substitute for him just as a boy wants to marry his mother or a substitute for her. The same-sex struggle may be transferred to the parental substitute or parent surrogate. In the case of Disney's "The Little Mermaid", Ursula competes with Ariel for the prized Prince Eric. It is Ursula, the mother figure, who is the false or substitute bride. She is the older mother who envies her young daughter's beauty. She wants to be young and attractive like her daughter. Through magic, she succeeds in transforming herself into a beautiful young woman and with the aid of Ariel's voice that she has obtained, she is able to dupe Eric into agreeing to marry her instead of Ariel.

Ursula is a gross and grotesque caricature of a *femme fatale*, another aspect of the original siren figure, and her seductive powers are considerable. At one point near the end of the movie, having gained possession of Triton's trident, she stirs up the waters sufficiently so as to raise Eric's sunken ship from the bottom of the sea to the surface, a notable symbolic resurrection. This eventually leads to Ursula's downfall as Eric deftly uses the jagged prow of his ship to ram Ursula and this frontal attack succeeds in penetrating Ursula sufficiently to destroy her. As she meets her death, images of cemeterial crosses formed from masts of the ship are prominent in the background. The phallic nature of Eric's improvised weapon has been recognized by several critics (Leadbetter and Wilson, 1993, p. 475; Trites, 1990–1991, p. 150). A more overt and less symbolic testament to Ursula's feminine charms lies in a very controversial, if brief, moment in the film. On board ship when Eric is about to marry Ursula (before the ceremony is interrupted at the last minute by Ariel's various animal helpers), the minister performing the marriage service is depicted as having an erection barely concealed by his pants. Since he is male, his arousal is presumably caused by the sexual allure of Ursula. This incident is so brief that it is difficult to see without stopping the film. Perhaps it was meant to be an inside joke by the Disney studio personnel who worked on the film although Disney's response was that some viewers misinterpreted a perfectly innocuous movement of the minister's knee. Another possible inside joke consists of a seemingly overtly penile-shaped turret centrally located on the castle depicted on the illustrated case cover of the original videocassette. Disney's apparent response was to replace this illustration on the cover of later releases of the video, totally removing all traces of a castle.

Ursula whose name derives from Ursa or bear—is there a play on a sexually mature woman's ability to "bear" children?—has the identity of an octopus. The word octopus consists of "octo" meaning "eight" and "pus" meaning foot. (The latter is, of course, the same morpheme contained in the name of Oedipus which means literally "swollen foot" or symbolically an erection.) Trites suggests that "Ursula seems to be an inverse Medusa figure. The snake-like appendages also make Ursula a perversion of femininity; her tentacles could be interpreted as eight phalluses" (1990-1991, p. 150). Her two male pet eels, Flotsam and Jetsam, who have visible sharp teeth and to whom she is very attached, also have phallic significance (cf. Otero, 1996, p. 270). But it turns out that Ursula's "penis envy" is not satisfied by her eight feet. Instead, she "covets the powers of the male phallus" as is suggested when she "lovingly caresses Triton's trident while he is holding it" stroking one of the tines with her fingers (Trites, 1990–1991, p. 150). It would seem that Ursula's agenda includes more than competing with Ariel for Eric. She is also engaged in a battle of the sexes with Triton.

When Ariel fails to get Eric to kiss her within the prescribed three-day period, she must, according to the legally binding contract she signed with Ursula, revert to being a mermaid. Her father Triton, realizing the sincerity of Ariel's love for Eric, decides to sacrifice himself for her sake and to take her place in the contract. Ursula is delighted as apparently she was more interested in unmanning Triton than in defeating Ariel. Triton reluctantly uses his trident to seal an agreement to trade places with Ariel. He then hands over the trident, the symbol of his power, whereupon he immediately shrinks into a shriveled shadow of himself to join other captive souls in Ursula's garden. The loss of the trident would constitute symbolic castration while the dramatic shrinking would appear to be symbolic detumescence. At this juncture all seems lost. The father king is trident-less and the villainous mother-figure Ursula is in complete control.

The castration theme is also repeated in subplot detail. Sebastian, the Caribbean crab, whom Triton originally assigned to watch over Ariel but who eventually becomes sympathetic to her desire to become human, is at one point chased by Prince Eric's French chef Louis who holds a huge cleaver, and later attacks the crab with a full arsenal of glistening sharp knives. Fortunately, he does not succeed in chopping off either of Sebastian's claws. He is shown, however, hacking the heads off fish and the castration imagery is thus dramatically intensified by the sight of dozens of decapitated fish surrounded by countless disembodied fish heads.

Ursula quickly utilizes her new-found power by rising up to gigantic proportions whereupon she emerges from the water, with a phallic projection from a now oversized crown driving apart Ariel and Prince Eric who are huddling together (Leadbeater and Wilson, 1993, p. 475). As a result of Ursula's expansion, Ariel gets sucked down into a vortex that with its cavernous form resembles her hidden cave under the sea. That is, Ariel is rendered helpless by being trapped in a womb-like enclosure

(Johansen, 1996, p. 216) whereas Ursula, once in possession of the trident, becomes instantly masculine, even to the extent of acquiring a deepened, clearly manly voice. Thus, the only powerful woman in the story fulfills her desire for supreme power by becoming masculine, both in actual presentation and symbolically (by gaining possession of both the crown with its unmistakable crenellated circle of vertical projections ending with sharp points and the potent trident). Ultimately, however, her usurpation of the male role is all for naught and the "unnatural" situation is "rectified" by her fatal re-feminization through a dramatic impalement.

One might well ask what is the thematic relationship, if any, between the figure of the mermaid and castration? Recall that in the original Andersen story, the sea witch cuts out the mermaid's tongue which feminists have correctly interpreted as symbolic castration. Dinnerstein suggested that the woman is perceived essentially as a castrated male, that is, as a human lacking the male penis; but there is another possible explanation for the linkage between the mermaid figure and castration. One could argue that the mermaid represents the fear of feminine power in general and the fear of unbridled sexual appetite in particular (Johnson, 1987, pp. 73–74). Certainly in Mediterranean cultures, the female is perceived as possessing a vagina which is threatening (sometimes portrayed by the addition of teeth—*vagina dentata*) which coupled with her presumed voracious sexual appetite constitutes a castratory danger to males. Narratives which include so-called "Poison damsels" (Motif F582; see Penzer, 1952), "Serpent damsel" (Motif F582.1), in which a woman has a serpent inside her vagina which comes out and kills her bridegrooms, or the *"vagina dentata"* (Motif F547.1.1; see Creed, 1993; Otero, 1996) play on this male fear. The film *Jaws* (1975) is another tale of a *vagina dentata* lurking in the sea.

Inasmuch as the mermaid has no vagina, with or without teeth, she is no threat. The phallic Ursula is, in contrast, a castrating female. Ursula as *vagina dentata* is signaled by a detail noticed by several feminist critics. "Ursula's palace is entered through the mouth opening of a skeletal animal, and the swimming entrant must traverse the long neck of the animal before penetrating the womb-like inner chamber where Ursula resides" (Trites, 1990–1991, p. 149). "To visit Ursula, Ariel must enter through the toothy jaws of a gigantic mouth, and swim through womb-like caves" (Sells, 1995, p. 184). In contrast, Ariel has a body innocent of any dental threat. The only hint is her mistaking a fork for a comb. The comb, along with the narcissistic mirror, traditionally have been the standard accoutrements of mermaids (Benwell and Waugh, 1961, pp. 137–139; Higgins, 1995, p. 40). As a comb, the fork's tines become metaphorical teeth placed in her hair, but Eric and his dinner companions soon civilize Ariel by teaching her the true nature of a fork. The sexual innuendo of the fork as comb would have been transparent to the Romans. The Latin word for comb "pecten" also meant the female pudenda (Phillpotts, 1980, p. 10) or pubic hair (Adams, 1982, p. 76).

There is another possible interpretation supporting the notion that Ariel must be castrated in order to become Prince Eric's bride. The mermaid's fishtail is not only a denial of the vagina, but it could symbolize a penis (Lederer, 1986, p. 251; Róheim, 1948, pp. 22, 33). If this is so, then Ariel's phallic attributes are somewhat analogous to those of Ursula with her serpentine octopus lower body tentacles. For Ariel to transform into a viable human female, she must lose her phallic fishtail. The castration of Ariel is further confirmed in the original Andersen story by the cutting out of her tongue. (Even though this detail was omitted from the Disney version, Ursula tosses a tongue of unknown origin into her brew designed to rob Ariel of her ability to speak, a witty literalization of the metaphor referring to the likely adverse effects caused by a "loose tongue.") Even the loss of Ariel's voice could be similarly construed according to Bunker's essay "The Voice as (Female) Phallus." Bunker does mention sirens and mermaids (1934, p. 411) but without reference to Andersen's "The Little Mermaid."

One could speculate that the male fear of castration by a female is transformed through inverse projection to the castration of females by males. The story in which the mermaid's tongue is cut out was, after all, written by a male Hans Christian Andersen and the Disney script was also written by men. The male bias of the Disney studio has been well established by feminists. The history of the male domination of women includes a series of imposed restrictions designed to curb female sexuality ranging from chastity belts to keeping unmarried girls under virtual house arrest behind secure walls. Another striking illustration of the male's fear of female sexuality is perhaps provided by the widespread practice of female genital mutilation, particularly prevalent in Africa. It is justified in part by the claim that the genital mutilation allegedly reduces women's sexual desire which purportedly would otherwise be out of control. The excision of the clitoris is sometimes followed by infibulation, which means that the initiate cannot have sexual intercourse until the stitched vagina is cut or torn open. One critic in speaking of the mermaid in the Andersen story even goes so far as to suggest that "her loss of a tongue may be the symbolic displacement of clitorectomy" (Dahlerup, 1990, p. 427). So since the mermaid imago herself is a male ideal of sexual allure without the dangerous castratory vagina dentata, it is not surprising that such an overt castration theme permeates "The Little Mermaid" film. The thematic linkage between mermaid and castration is explicit in a striking bit of American material culture. In the late 1920s, a curious fishing lure appeared as a novelty item. As reported by the late Gershon Legman (1975, p. 433), it consisted of "a naked-breasted mermaid with a three-pronged hook emanating from her pubis." Gleefully thinking of her prospective triumph over King Triton, Ursula speaks of looking forward to seeing "him wriggle like a worm on a hook." The phallic nature of fish caught by fish hooks continues to be obvious as indicated by the bragging of fishermen who carefully measure and weigh their trophies, sometimes even mounting them over fireplaces in their game rooms. The repeated vandalism of the famous statue of "The Little Mermaid," the veritable symbol of the city of Copenhagen, also confirms the association of castration with the mermaid. For the vandalism, presumably carried out by males, often involves decapitation, an act that not only connotes castration but which may also suggest defloration, that is, destroying a virginal maiden head.

Whereas a young girl can be controlled by female genital mutilation or by depicting her as mermaid, the mature female remains a threat. When Eric succeeds in penetrating Ursula with the jagged prow of his raised ship, this not only destroys the evil sea witch, but results in her dropping the trident which fortuitously falls to the bottom of the sea right near the shriveled Triton. Symbolically, Ursula has been so utterly feminized, not to say decimated, by Eric's phallic attack, that she can no longer retain possession of the powerful trident. Triton regains his trident, swells to attain his previous imposing and muscular build, and is then empowered to set everything straight.

The role of the trident in Disney's "The Little Mermaid" has not been sufficiently noted by critics. The word literally means "three teeth" and both the number three and teeth have phallic significance (Freud, 1915–1916, pp. 163–165). The trident turns out to be crucial in terms of the male reworking of an Electral fantasy. Early in the film when Triton learns about Ariel's secret grotto where she stores her human artifacts, he visits her there and destroys the chamber and its contents with his powerful trident. Symbolically speaking, a secret chamber or garden or other hiding place of a young girl is an obvious representation of her vagina. The entrance to the chamber is a tubular tunnel marked by striations that would appear to resemble the transverse ridges of a vaginal wall. Inside the chamber Ariel flirts with and sings to a lifelike statue of Prince Eric (Leadbeater and Wilson, 1993, p. 474), commissioned for Prince Eric from Grimsby, which was salvaged from the wreckage of the destroyed ship. (It is curious that the statue of "The Little Mermaid" in Copenhagen harbor was sculpted by Edvard Eriksen and that might partially account for the choice of the name Eric for the prince.) The statue of Prince Eric, intended as a nuptial gift, portrays him as about to draw his sword, presumably suggesting the impending penetration following marriage. King Triton later obliterates the statue with his trident, just as the mermaid figurehead on Eric's ship was destroyed by a stormy sea. The discovery and wholesale destruction of her secret hideout foreshadows her eventual loss of virginity. As Triton wields this instrument symbolic of male power, it becomes illuminated, perhaps even implying heat. The illuminated trident is somewhat reminiscent of the remarkable extensible light sabers utilized in *Star Wars* for Oedipal father-son duels.

The "hot" trident reappears near the end of the movie when Triton relents and agrees to allow Ariel to leave his watery domain to join the world of humans on land. Still a mermaid, Ariel needs human legs and the requisite interstitial female genitals in order to become Eric's bride. Triton accomplishes this transformation with one flick of his mighty trident. Poof! The mermaid's tail disappears and is replaced by human legs. It is the father who gives his daughter, his favorite daughter, the necessary sexual parts which will allow her to marry Eric, and consummate the marriage properly. One may recall that when Ariel returned "in love" after her initial encounters with humans (including Prince Eric), she presented a flower to her father. This blatant prefiguration of defloration is thus a definite daughter-father matter. Just in case the audience should miss this floral sign, it is immediately followed by Ariel's plucking petals in a version of the well-known divinatory custom "He loves me, he loves me not" (Mieder, 1985). Completion of this literal and symbolic defloration ritual ends with Ariel picking the last petal exclaiming triumphantly "He loves me."

The essential Electral nature of the entire plot is confirmed by the very last words of the film. After finally being kissed by Eric at the conclusion of the marriage ceremony, Ariel embraces her father and whispers intimately, "I love you, Daddy." While smiling tenderly at him, she slowly backs up and then blows him a kiss. The final scene shows Prince Eric and Ariel's ship sailing off towards the arc of a rainbow, a rainbow magically produced by father Triton with one sweep of his illuminated "hot" trident. The ship's entrance into the semi-circular image is yet one more sign of consummation of the marriage on the wedding night. Another such symbol is the French chef's cutting the white wedding cake into two halves with his cleaver. A white wedding cake is a standard symbol of a virginal bride and the plunging of a knife (often nowadays a joint venture involving the hands of both bride and groom) into the cake symbolizes the nuptial defloration (Charsley, 1992, p. 126). In American wedding ritual, the knife poised for the initial insertion into the usually round white cake is typically one of the principal post-wedding photographic highlights. In the Disney film, the bifurcation of the cake into two halves could also represent in microcosm the successful transformation of Ariel's monolithic fish tail into two legs.

We can well imagine that readers hostile to psychoanalytic thought will say that they saw Disney's "The Little Mermaid" and that they never once thought of most, if any, of the symbolic elements discussed above. Perhaps the Disney staff members who worked on the film night respond similarly. Disney films are on the surface conspicuously wholesome family entertainment with nary a hint of sexuality. Mickey and Minnie Mouse never have sex; nor do Donald and Daisy Duck (Berland, 1982, pp. 96, 103). But our analysis is concerned with the latent and not the manifest content of the "The Little Mermaid." We would argue generally that Disney's choice of plots for cartoon treatment is almost certainly made without awareness of unconscious symbolic elements. Why would Disney have chosen to make a movie, for example, about the masturbatory rubbing of a magic lamp that produces a wish-granting genie? (Aladdin is Aarne-Thompson tale type 561.) For that matter, the Electral plot has proven itself in earlier successful Disney films. "Show White" (Aarne-Thompson tale type 709) tells of a wicked stepmother's attempt to kill the heroine and there is a competition between them as to who of the two is the most beautiful. Similarly, "Cinderella" (Aarne-Thompson tale type 510A) involves a girl's struggle with a stepmother and in some versions (AT 510B) a motif in which a father wants to marry his own daughter, a clear inverse projection of a daughter's wish to marry her own father. In Disney films subsequent to "The Little Mermaid", the Electral component continues: "Beauty and the Beast" (Aarne-Thompson tale type 425C) and "Mulan" both concern a father-daughter constellation in which the daughter, against the father's wishes, insists on imperiling herself to protect her father. Indeed, as "Pocahontas" concludes, she elects to sacrifice her romantic relationship in order to stay in her village and assist her father in maintaining peace.

Disney has found a sure-fire formula for success, namely a cartoon-rendering of the Electra Complex. We suggest that the "The Little Mermaid" is just a modern version of this tried and true plot, with male chauvinist patriarchal values superimposed upon it. A sexy young girl who wears a shell bra which reveals more than it conceals (Bendix, 1993, p. 287; O'Brien, 1996, p. 173) is given female genitals by her father so that she can marry a prince who has destroyed her rival mother surrogate by a heroic act of penetration. So the girl enjoys the Electral fantasy of seeing a mother figure eliminated and wedding the man her mother surrogate was about to marry, but at the same time the power of the trident (and a ship's prow) remains the exclusive property of males (Triton and Eric).

The fact that "The Little Mermaid" is readily available on videotape has greatly increased the dissemination of this psychologically loaded narrative way beyond its original movie-theater audience. Accordingly, this male-constructed Electral fantasy, with its powerful embedded patriarchal overlay, is likely to continue to influence the emotional development of all the young girls who see it and identify with Ariel. At the same time, it may also impact upon little boys. Although the story is certainly nominally about a female mermaid (Johansen, 1996, p. 220), the recurring themes of castration and the fear of the phallic female no doubt reflect the unconscious anxieties of the males (Andersen and Disney writers) who created the story. In that light, Disney's "The Little Mermaid" would appear to encapsulate critical emotional issues for both girls and boys. This may serve to help explain the enormous popularity of such a unique male construction of an Electral fantasy.

References Cited

Aarne, A. and S. Thompson (1961) *The Types of the Folktale.* Second Revision. Helsinki: Academia Scientiarum Fennica.

Adams, J. N. (1982) *The Latin Sexual Vocabulary.* London: Duckworth.

Almendral Oppermann, A. I. (1992) Existencia y poder de las figuras acuáticas femeninas en la cultural popular centroeuropea. Su significación mitológico-religiosa, *Revista de dialectologia y tradiciones populares* 47, pp. 217–240.

Baggesen, S. (1967a) Individuation eller frelse?, *Kritik* 1, pp. 50–77.

Baggesen, S. (1967b) Replik til Eigil Nyborg, *Kritik* 2: 129–134.

Banse, K. (1990) Mermaids—Their Biology, Culture, and Demise, *Limnology and Oceanography* 35(1), pp. 148–153.

Bech, H. (1998) A Dung Beetle in Distress: Hans Christian Andersen Meets Karl Maria Kertbeny, Geneva, 1860: Some Notes on the Archaeology of Homosexuality and the Importance of Tuning. *Journal of Homosexuality* 35(3/4): 139–161.

Bendix, R. (1993) Seashell Bra and Happy End: Disney's Transformations of *The Little Mermaid*, *Fabula* 34, pp. 280–290.

Benwell, G. and A. Waugh (1961) *Sea Enchantress: The Tale of the Mermaid and her Kin.* London: Hutchinson.

Berland, D. I. (1982) Disney and Freud: Walt Meets the Id, *Journal of Popular Culture* 15, pp. 93–104.

Bondeson, J. (1999) *The Feejee Mermaid and Other Essays in Natural and Unnatural History.* Ithaca: Cornell University Press.

Bouillet, J. (1958) Symbolisme d'un Mythe, *Aesculape* 41, pp. 3–62.

Bredsdorff, E. (1975) *Hans Christian Andersen: The Story of His Life and Work 1805–75.* New York: The Noonday Press.

Broendsted, G. K. (1965) *Havfruens Saga: En literaer-kunsthistoriskorientering.* Copenhagen: G.E.C Gads Forlag.

Bunker, H. A. (1934) The Voice as (Female) Phallus, *Psychoanalytic Quarterly* 3, pp. 391–429.

Burnell, F. S. (1949) Ino and Her Veil, *Folklore* 60, pp. 201–207.

Charsley, S. r. (1992) *Wedding Cakes and Cultural History.* London: Routledge.

Consoli, S. (1974) Le Mythe de la Sirène: Variantes, fantasmes sous-jacents et implications psychopathologiques, *L'Evolution Psychiatrique* 39, pp. 63–89.

Consoli, S. (1980) *La candeur d'un monstre: essai psychanalytique sur le mythede la sirène.* Paris: Le Centurion.

Creed, B. (1993) Medusa's Head: The *Vagina Dentata* and Freudian Theory, in *The Monstrous-Feminine: Film, Feminism, Psychoanalysis.* London: Routledge, pp. 105–121.

Dahlerup, P. (1990) *The Little Mermaid* Deconstructed, *Scandinavian Studies* 62, pp. 418–428.

Deonna, W. (1928) La Sirène, Femme-Poisson, *Revue Archéologique*, Cinquième Série, 27, pp. 18–25.

Dinnerstein, D. (1967) "The Little Mermaid" and the Situation of the Girl, *Contemporary Psychoanalysis* 3(2). pp. 104–112.

Duve, A. (1967) *Symbolikken i H.C. Andersens Eventyr.* Oslo: Psychopress.

Engel, B. (1988) Wandlungssymbolik in Andersens Märchen "Die kleine Meerjungfrau," *Praxis der Kinderpsychologie und Kinderpsychiatrie* 37, pp. 374–378.

Faral, E. (1953) La Queue de Poisson des Sirènes, *Romania* 74, pp. 433–506.

Freud, S. (1915–1916) Symbolism in Dreams, in *Standard Edition*, Vol. 15. London: Hogarth Press, pp. 149–169.
Freud, S. (1920) The Psychogenesis of a Case of Homosexuality in a Woman, in *Standard Edition*, Vol. 18. London: Hogarth Press, pp. 147–172.
Freud, S. (1932) Femininity, in *Standard Edition*, Vol. 22. London: Hogarth Press, pp. 112–135.
Golden, S. (1998) *Slaying the Mermaid: Women and the Culture of Sacrifice*. New York: Three Rivers Press.
Goodman, A. S. (1983) The Extraordinary Being: Death and the Mermaid in Baroque Literature, *Journal of Popular Culture* 17(3), pp. 32–48.
Griffith, J. (1984) Personal Fantasy in Andersen's Fairy Tales, *Kansas Quarterly* 16(3), pp. 81–88.
Grönbech, B. (1996) Weltbild und Kunst in den Märchen von H.C. Andersen, in L. Petzoldt (ed.), *Folk Narrative and Worldview*. Frankfurt: Peter Lang, pp. 219–225.
Hansen, A. (1901) H.C. Andersen. Beweis seiner Homosexualität, *Jahrbuch für sexuelle Zwischenstufen mit besonderer Berücksichtigung der Homosexualität* 3, pp. 203–230.
Hastings, A. W. (1993) Moral Simplification in Disney's *The Little Mermaid*, *The Lion and the Unicorn* 17, pp. 83–92.
Helweg, H. (1927) *H.C. Andersen: En Psykiatrisk Studie*. Copenhagen: H. Hagerups Forlag.
Helweg, H. (1929) H.C. Andersen und die Behauptung seiner Homosexualität, *Zeitschrift für die gesamte Neurologie und Psychiatrie* 118, pp. 777–788.
Higgins, J. (1995) *Irish Mermaids: Sirens, Temptresses and their Symbolism in Art, Architecture and Folklore*. Galway: Crow's Rock Press.
Holbek, B. (1990) Hans Christian Andersen's Use of Folktales, in Morten Noejgaard et al. (eds), *The Telling of Stories: Approaches to a Traditional Craft: A Symposium*. Odense: Odense University Press, pp. 165–182.
Ingwersen, N. and F. Ingwersen (1990) A Folktale/Disney Approach, *Scandinavian Studies* 62, pp. 412–415.
Johansen, J. D. (1996) The Merciless Tragedy of Desire: An Interpretation of H.C. Andersen's "Den lille Havfrue," *Scandinavian Studies* 68, pp. 203–241.
Johnson, C. (1987) The Fate of the Legendary Mermaid in Modern Cartoon Jokes, *Folklore Forum* 20, pp. 61–84.
Jung, C. G. (1975) *Critique of Psychoanalysis*. Princeton: Princeton University Press.
Leadbeater, B. J. and G. L. Wilson (1993) Flipping Their Fins For A Place To Stand: 19th- and 20th-Century Mermaids, *Youth & Society* 24, pp. 466–486.
Leclercq-Marx, J. (1997) *La Sirène dans la pensée et dans l'art de l'Antiquité et du Moyen Age*. Brussels: Académie royale de Belgique.
Lederer, W. (1986) *The Kiss of the Snow Queen: Hans Christian Andersen and Man's Redemption by Woman*. Berkeley: University of California Press.
Legman, G. (1975) *No Laughing Matter*. New York: Breaking Point.
Liberati, A. (1995) Sirene. Immagini di un archetipo fra XIX e XX secolo, *Ricerche di Storia dell'arte* 57, pp. 23–37.
Mäeenpää-Reenkola, E. (1989) Pieni merenneito—eräs itsetuhosyndrooma [The Little Mermaid: A syndrome of self-destructive behavior], *Psykologia* 24, pp. 345–349.
Marót, K. (1958) The Sirens, *Acta Ethnographica* 7, pp. 1–60.
Mieder, W. (1985) Modern Variants of the Daisy Oracle: He Loves Me, He Loves Me Not, *Midwestern Journal of Language and Folklore* 11, pp. 65–115.
Moog, H. (ed.) (1987) *Die Wasserfrau*. Köln: Eugen Diederichs Verlag.
Nybo, G. (1990) A Synopsis, *Scandinavian Studies* 62, pp. 416–418.
Nyborg, E. (1962) *Den Indre Linie i H.C. Andersens Eventyr: En Psykologisk Studie*. Gyldendal: Nordisk Forlag.
Nyborg, E. (1967) Psykologien og ny-kritikken, *Kritik* 2, pp. 116–128.
O'Brien, P. C. (1996) The Happiest Films on Earth: A Textual and Contextual Analysis of Walt Disney's *Cinderella* and *The Little Mermaid*, *Women's Studies in Communications* 19, pp. 155–183.

Otero, S. (1996) "Fearing Our Mothers": An Overview of the Psychoanalytic Theories Concerning the Vagina Dentata Motif F547.1.1, *The American Journal of Psychoanalysis* 56, pp. 269–288.
Penzer, N. M. (1952) *Poison-Damsels and Other Essays in Folklore and Anthropology*. London: Charles J. Sawyer.
Phillpotts, B. (1980) *Mermaids*. New York: Ballantine Books.
Propp, V. (1968) *Morphology of the Folktale*. Austin: University of Texas Press.
Rachewiltz, S. de (1987) *De sirenibus: an inquiry into Sirens from Homer to Shakespeare*. New York: Garland.
Ringblom, H. (1997) Om H.C. Andersens påståede homosexualitet, *Anderseniana*, pp. 41–58.
Roebling, I. (ed.) (1991) *Sehnsucht und Sirene: Vierzehn Abhandlungen zu Wasserphantasien*. Pfaffenweiler: Centaurus.
Róheim, G. (1948) The Song of the Sirens, *Psychiatric Quarterly* 22, pp. 18–44.
Róheim, G. (1953) *The Gates of the Dream*. New York: International Universities Press.
von Rosen, W. (1978–1981) Venskabets mysterier, *Anderseniana* 3, pp. 167–214.
Sells, L. (1995) Where Do the Mermaids Stand? Voice and Body in *The Little Mermaid*, in E. Bell, L. Haas and L. Sells (eds.), *From Mouse to Mermaid: The Politics of Film, Gender, and Culture*. Bloomington: Indiana University Press, pp. 175–192.
Shainess, N. (1984) *Sweet Suffering: Woman as Victim*. Indianapolis: Bobbs-Merrill Company.
Shepard, K. (1940) *The Fish-Tailed Monster in Greek and Etruscan Art*. New York: Privately Printed.
Soracco, S. (1990) A Psychoanalytic Approach, *Scandinavian Studies* 62, pp. 407–412.
Spears, R. A. (1990) *Forbidden American English*. Lincolnwood: Passport Books.
Stuby, A. M. (1992) *Liebe, Tod und Wasserfrau: Mythen de Weiblichen in der Literatur*. Wiesbaden: Westdeutscher Verlag.
Thomsen, U. (1990) A Structuralist Approach, *Scandinavian Studies* 62, pp. 403–407.
Touchefeu-Meynier, O. (1962) De quand date la Sirène-poisson?, *Bulletin de l'Association Guillaume Budé* 21, pp. 450–459.
Tristaon, M. (1601) A Treatise of Brasil, written by a Portugall which had long lived there, in Samuel Purchas (ed.), *Pilgrimes*. London: William Stansby (1625), pp. 1289–1320.
Trites, R. (1990–1991) Disney's Sub/Version of Andersen's *The Little Mermaid*, *Journal of Popular Film & Television*, 18, pp. 145–152.
Tseëlon, E. (1995) *The Little Mermaid*: An Icon of Woman's Condition in Patriarchy, and the Human Condition of Castration, *International Journal of Psycho-Analysis* 76, pp. 1017–1030.
Waugh, A. (1960) The Folklore of the Merfolk, *Folklore* 71, pp. 73–84.
Zipes, J. (1993) *The Trials & Tribulations of Little Red Riding Hood*. Second Edition. New York: Routledge.

5

Bloody Mary in the Mirror

A RITUAL REFLECTION OF PRE-PUBESCENT ANXIETY

One of the most disheartening aspects of folkloristics, the scientific study of folklore, is the persistent lack of analysis or interpretation. It is not just popularizers who churn out anthology after anthology of "texts only" without attention to context or possible meaning(s) of such texts, but the academic folklorists themselves, who despite pretentious definitional debates about the wisdom of continuing to use the term "folklore" or exaggerated claims of the importance of reporting folklore as "performed"—even to the point of calling this approach "performance theory"—what exactly is the "theory" supposedly underlying "performance theory"???—do little more than report folkloristic texts totally devoid of the slightest hint of thoughtful commentary. Yes, certainly the legitimate concern for performance has resulted in more accurate reporting of texts, but it is nonetheless hard to find instances where such increased accuracy has yielded actual insights with respect to the meaning or significance of a folkloristic event.

I would like to illustrate this disappointing facet of folkloristics by examining one single traditional ritual found in American folklore. (It has also been reported in Newfoundland [Hiscock 1996].) After surveying what little is known about the ritual, I will propose an interpretation of it which I believe will make perfectly clear what the ritual is all about.

In 1976, Mary and Herbert Knapp, in their anthology of American children's folklore, devote a whole paragraph in a general discussion of what they term "Scaries" to the following item:

> "One child told us she was always too chicken to summon Mary Worth. She said, 'I knew I'd really be scared.' And really being scared is no fun.
> A child summons Mary Worth, alias Bloody Mary, alias Mary Jane, by going into the bathroom alone at night, turning out the lights, staring into the mirror, and repeating "Mary Worth," softly but distinctly, forty-seven times. She comes at you out of the mirror, with a knife in her hand and a wart on her nose. Never when we read Mary Worth comic strips did we dream that the respectable busybody was moonlighting as a mirror witch!" (1976:242).

Here we have most of the primary elements of this ritual: a child, almost always a girl, goes into a bathroom at night (or at school in the dark) and repeats the name Mary in some form which supposedly results in a frightening creature named Mary emerging from out of the bathroom mirror.

Folklorist Simon J. Bronner in his 1988 *American Children's Folklore* included an entire page of discussion of what he called "Mary Worth Rituals." He describes the ritual as "a girls' tradition common in elementary school" which invokes "atmosphere of the seance" (1988:168). Whoever the "Mary" figure is, Bronner indicates that the participants are "Huddled typically in a bathroom with the lights turned off" and that they "have to really 'believe' in her, or else she won't appear" (1988:168). In his notes to his texts, Bronner remarks that "Bloody Mary" is yet another name for variations of 'Mary Worth' rituals" (1988:266, n.24). One of the five texts Bronner reports—collected from a male informant from Middletown, Pennsylvania, in 1984—is as follows:

> Bloody Mary was a character who was murdered in the woods behind Pine Road Elementary School. To call her ghost, girls go in the bathroom and prick their fingers with a pin to draw a drop of blood. Then they press the two droplets of blood together and say "We believe in Bloody Mary" ten times with their eyes shut. Then upon opening their eyes they look into the bathroom mirror. The image of Bloody Mary's face would appear in the mirror. She was said to have been a young girl with long hair, very pale

skin, and blood running down her face from a large cut in her forehead (1988:168–169).

Bronner offers no more in the way of interpretation than did the Knapps, but his text includes an element not found in the Knapps' brief report, namely, the presence of blood. It is precisely this element which turns out to be critical with respect to interpreting the ritual. Though Bronner provides little insight into the Bloody Mary custom he does at least refer in his notes to the only in-depth study of it, an essay by folklorist Janet Langlois entitled " 'Mary Whales, I Believe in You': Myth and Ritual Subdued" which had appeared in *Indiana Folklore* in 1978. Folklorist Linda Dégh evidently thought enough of Langlois's essay to reprint it in her edited anthology *Indiana Folklore: A Reader* in 1980.

Langlois bases her discussion of "Bloody Mary" upon some seventeen excellent texts, twelve of which were collected in Indianapolis in 1973. (The other texts came from the Indiana University folklore archives.) For some reason, she insisted upon calling the custom a "game" although she was well aware of the fact that the ritual was often connected with a "legend." Indeed, Langlois's principal concern in her essay was to seek to illuminate the long-standing and vexing question of the relationship between "myth" and "ritual." (For references to myth-ritual theory, see Segal, 1980, Grimes 1985, and Ackerman 1991.)

The basic issue in this age-old chicken-and-egg debate is whether ritual derives from myth or whether myth stems from initial ritual. Neither possibility is really satisfactory in terms of explaining ultimate origins. If myth comes from ritual, where did the ritual come from? And if ritual derives from myth, where did the original myth come from? In any case, Langlois interviewed no fewer than eighty students at Holy Angels, an experimental Catholic elementary school for African-American children in northwest Indianapolis. Of these eighty informants, approximately twenty knew the "Mary Whales thing" and about half of that number had actively participated in the "legend/game" (1978:6). Not surprisingly, Langlois reluctantly concluded that "neither the legend nor the game is primary for this particular group" and that "it is not possible to establish in which direction the transformation goes' (1978:9). Although Langlois may have failed in her primary goal of trying to resolve or at least illuminate the myth-ritual controversy, she did make a valuable observation about the ritual. It has to do with the importance of the mirror. Speaking of the function of the mirror, Langlois remarks that "it literally reflects the identification of the participants with the revenant. In normal situations, when any of the girls looks in the mirror, she sees herself; in reports of the game-playing, she sees Mary Whales, or at least, expects to. In a sense, then Mary Whales becomes the girl's own reflection" (1978). I believe Langlois is absolutely correct in this observation, but brilliant though it may be, it does not really explain the underlying meaning of the ritual.

Folklorist Jan Brunvand was sufficiently impressed by Langlois's comment that he referred to it in his own three-page discussion of "I Believe in Mary Worth" to quip that it "should give Freudians something to chew on" (1986:81). However, unfortunately, Brunvand did not elaborate further. In fact, he throws up his hands in despair. ". . . So what does it all have to do with the kindly Mary Worth of the comics? Nothing, as far as I can tell . . . so the precise origin of "I Believe in Mary Worth" cannot be determined" (1986:82. For further discussion of "America's favorite grandmother, Mary Worth," a soap-opera comic strip that first appeared in the early 1930s, see Horn 1977:170 and 1996:197–198.)

It is clear that folklorists Bronner, Langlois and Brunvand certainly know about the "Bloody Mary" ritual, but it is equally obvious that its basic underlying significance, if any, seems to have eluded them. And this is exactly what I meant by my opening complaint that there is a persistent and consistent lack of analysis or interpretation in folkloristics. Moreover, if folklorists themselves are unwilling or unable to interpret folklore, they can scarcely blame others for holding the discipline in such low intellectual repute.

What exactly does the reflection of Bloody Mary mean? Or is it essentially mean**ing**less? And why does the ritual almost invariably take place **in a bathroom**? What is the significance, if any, of the names: Mary Worth, Mary Whales, Bloody Mary? No analysis of an item of folklore can be deemed complete unless it can explain **all** of the traits or details of that item.

There are important clues in the texts reported by Langlois, clues which have thus far not been adequately explored by folklorists. For example, more than half of the texts she elicited herself (as opposed to those on file in the Indiana University folklore archives) were combined with the "Vanishing Hitchhiker". So one additional question to be asked is why is the "Bloody Mary" ritual attached to this particular legend? Let us consider the first text presented by Langlois. It was collected from twelve-year old Anna L. in February of 1973:

> Q. Have you heard about a dead girl called Mary Whales or Mary Worth?
> A. Yes, I've heard about Mary Whales. Well, to tell you the truth, I don't know much about her. All I know is that she stood on [the] corner when it rained and she had a long white dress on. and when someone stopped to give her a ride she would disappear in the back seat and just leave a wet spot with blood on the seat, and she wouldn't be in [the] car anymore (1978:13).

What is noteworthy about this abbreviated legend is the reference to a "wet spot with blood" in the backseat of the car. There are numerous recorded versions of this popular legend (Motif E 332.3.3.1, The Vanishing Hitchhiker; for more than one hundred references, see Bennett and Smith 1993:338). But in those versions where an object is left behind as "proof" of the truth value of the legend, that object can be "a purse, a suitcase, a blanket, a sweater, a scarf or some other item of clothing, or simply footprints or water spots in the car" (Brunvand 1981:27). There is no mention of blood at all. Wet spots or footprints in the car are "often mentioned in connection with American vanishing hitchhikers," notes Brunvand, the acknowledged authority on this and other modern legends, but "Why, or how, a spirit would get wet feet is not explained, though" (Brunvand 1993:251). The wetness motif is explained by neither the folk nor folklorist Brunvand.

By now the astute reader may already suspect what the possible significance of the "Bloody Mary" ritual might be. But for those who may still be in the dark, let me present a small but representative sampling of 10 texts from more than seventy-five reports, collected in 1996 unless otherwise noted, from my undergraduate folklore students at the University of California, Berkeley.[1]

Text 1:
Bloody Mary
During recess at school, you go into the girls' bathroom. Your friends wait outside because only [one] person is allowed in at a time. One girl stands at the

Bloody Mary in the Mirror   81

door to turn out the lights once you're positioned in front of the mirror. Once the lights are out, you close your eyes and turn around three times. Then you open them and stare straight into the mirror and chant, "Bloody Mary, show your fright. Show your fright this starry night." You have to chant slowly so she has time to come from the spirit world. Then you wait to see her face. Once you see her, you have to run out of the bathroom where your friends are waiting. If you've sinned or done anything evil in your life then you will have three scratches of blood on your cheek.

(Learned in the third grade in 1983 at Apollo Elementary School in Bossier City, Louisiana by the female collector, age 20)

Text 2:
  A bunch of us young girls went into the bathroom to call Bloody Mary. We turned off the lights, turned around 5 times chanting "Bloody Mary" over and over, then stopped quickly and looked in the mirror. We were supposed to look for a headless female in a white gown with a bloody knife in one hand and her head in the other.

(Learned in California by a female, age 20, when she was between the ages of ten and twelve)

Text 3:
  A group of girls usually go into a dark room where a mirror is present. Then everyone starts chanting "Bloody Mary" until it appears. A woman's bloody face will appear on the mirror.

(Learned by a nineteen-year-old Mexican-American female in Riverbank, California, when she was in the sixth grade [circa 1989])

Text 4:
  Okay, you go into the bathroom and you turn out the lights and you turn around three times and you say "Bloody Mary, Bloody Mary, Bloody Mary" and then Bloody Mary's head is supposed to appear on the mirror.

(Learned by a sixteen-year-old Chinese-American female as a sixth-grader when she attended slumber parties in Palos Verdes in southern California)

Text 5:

If you go in to a bathroom mirror every night for three nights, and you say "Bloody Mary" three times, then the first night a spot of blood appears and the second night, it's a little bigger, and the third night, it's supposed to be a woman's face.

(Collected in 1994 from a 22-year-old Irish-American female who learned it at a slumber party in Los Altos, California, in 1979, when she was a second grader)

Text 6:

To make Bloody Mary appear, you look into a mirror at midnight and chant "Bloody Mary" three times. You are then supposed to see your own bloodied face in the reflection.

(Collected from a 23-year-old female who learned it in sixth grade in Fairfield, California)

Text 7:

When I was in grade school (about fifth grade), I would go into the girls' bathroom at St. Thomas Aquinas school [in Monterey Park, California] with two or three of my friends to see Bloody Mary. We turned off the lights, approached the four-foot-wide mirror, and sprinkled water on the mirror. After the sprinkling, we chanted, "Bloody Mary" three times in hopes of seeing her in the mirror. Then we flushed all of the toilets in the stalls and ran out of the bathroom. Bloody Mary's mark would appear later on in the day through bleeding. For example, after I had completed the Bloody Mary ritual, I went to play frisbee during recess. In trying to catch the frisbee, I jammed my index finger, causing it to bleed. All of the girls who had done the Bloody Mary ritual with me attributed the bleeding to Bloody Mary.

(Collected from a female, age 20)

Text 8:

It can be any time of day, but you usually do it at night. You go into the bathroom—the hot water has to be on—you turn on the hot water full blast—and the bathroom has to have a mirror. Then you flush the toilet and as you're flushing the toilet, you say, "Bloody Mary, Bloody Mary, Bloody Mary"—three times you say "Bloody Mary" and you turn three times while you're saying it, and then you look in the mirror and some people say you see Bloody Mary . . . If you see her, she haunts your house.

(Collected in 1995 from a 9-year-old female who learned the custom in the second grade at the Hamlin School for Girls in San Francisco)

Text 9:
"Bloody Mary"
You go into the bathroom at school, turn out the lights, and close the door. You can go by yourself or with two or three friends. I'm not positive, but I think boys can do it too—if they want to. You light some red candles, like about three, and you put them in front of you in a triangle, two on a side and one in the front. Then you keep on chanting "Bloody Mary" like about three times or something. You're sitting there and looking at the water in the toilet and chanting. And they say she will appear, her face in the water. Then you have a weird reaction or something and she pulls you down into the toilet and flushes your head down the toilet. And you never come back or something.

(Collected from an 11-year-old Vietnamese-American female who learned it in third grade, in 1992, at Hellyer Elementary School in San Jose, California)

Text 10:
When I was in the 3rd, 4th, and 5th grades, many of the girls celebrated their birthdays (turning age 9, 10, 11) with a slumber party. I remember the game being played a few different ways. The idea was that you go into the bathroom alone and the light would be off, or there would be a candle or flashlight so that it would be barely visible in the bathroom. Then you were supposed to chant "Bloody Mary, Bloody Mary, Bloody Mary" as you look in the mirror. After you say "Bloody Mary" three times, there were a couple of things that could happen:
1) An image of a woman covered with blood would appear in the mirror.
2) You see your own reflection in the mirror but the mirror would soon be covered with blood so that it looked like you were covered with blood. At this point the girls would either run out of the bathroom screaming, or at some parties I remember the girls had to flush the toilet before they could come out. I think the toilet flushing was supposed to make the image go away, but no one

ever stayed in the bathroom long enough to see anything disappear. As soon as they pushed the toilet lever, they would run out scared and screaming.

The other version of Bloody Mary I remember goes like this: You say "Bloody Mary" three times, in a dark bathroom, but this time instead of looking at a mirror, you look at the toilet. After you finish the chant, the toilet water was supposed to turn red, or bloody, and then you had to flush the toilet in order to come out. Or, after the chant, you flush the toilet and as the toilet is flushing, the water turns red.

(Collected from a 21-year-old Korean-American female who learned it in Downey, California, in 1978)

These ten texts should suffice to demonstrate both the traditonality and the gamut of variation of the Bloody Mary ritual. Moreover, it should be abundantly clear that this girls' ritual has something to do with the onset of the first menses. The dramatic change from girlhood to womanhood is signaled physiologically by this catamenial condition. No one has stated this any more succinctly than anthropologist Margaret Mead: "The girl's first menstruation marks a dividing-line between childhood and womanhood. Whatever any given culture may have done in patterning this event, no recorded culture has ever patterned it out of existence" (1955:136).

The beginning of puberty is marked in many cultures by various formal initiation rituals, often in the case of females the ritual consisting of some form of enforced seclusion. A good portion of the discussion of menstruation folklore tends to concentrate on the diverse rituals and customs connected with this event (cf. Crawfurd 1915, Novak 1916, Voselmann 1935, Delaney, Lupton, and Toth 1977:22–30, Malmberg 1982, 1991). In American culture, there is no such formal ritual, but I suggest that the "Bloody Mary" ritual serves an analogous function for pre-pubescent American girls. One study of attitudes found among premenarchal girls reported that "the most frequent response was that of menstruation being exciting since it is related to growing up" (Williams 1980:40). Certainly the Bloody Mary ritual evokes feelings of excitement on the part of participants, excitement tinged with fear and apprehension as well.

There are a number of reasons why a menstrual interpretation of the Bloody Mary ritual makes sense. The ages of the young girls who participate in the ritual run from seven to twelve. According to one authority, the average American girl first experiences menarche at age 12 and 1/2 (Delaney, Lupton and Toth 1977:42). The Bloody Mary ritual in that context would appear to be an anticipatory ritual, essentially warning girls of what to expect upon attaining puberty.

The interpretation here proposed would certainly explain why the ritual invariably takes place **in a bathroom** and why there is such an explicit and repeated emphasis on **the sudden appearance of blood**. Another seemingly curious detail in some versions (texts 7, 8, 9, and 10) involve the flushing of one or more toilets. Inasmuch as one of the greatest fears of newly pubescent girls concerns the potentially embarrassing prospect of blood "showing," care is taken to ensure that any expelled blood from the urinogenital area be wiped off the body and flushed down a toilet. Sometimes, the pad or tampon may also be disposed of in the same fashion. The point is that the **flushing of a toilet** can easily be understood in the context of a menstrual interpretation of the Bloody Mary ritual.

There are other elements of the ritual which may also be illuminated by the theory proposed. The name "Mary" seems to be a constant whether it is Bloody Mary, Mary Worth, Mary Worthington, Mary Lou, Mary Jane (Brunvand 1986:81). The question is why! There could be an allusion to the Virgin Mary here—the ritual does occur frequently in Catholic elementary schools. Virginity is still an issue for young girls, especially when the risk of pregnancy is understood as a concomitant feature of pubescence. In addition, the vowel in the name "Mary" as pronounced in some American dialects of English is the same vowel as in the verb "marry." Part of the culturally defined transition from girlhood to womanhood entails the expectation that one day marriage might occur. The headlessness of Mary in some versions (text 2) might be a reference to Mary, Queen of Scots (1542–1587) who was in fact beheaded by order of Queen Elizabeth. However, it is by no means certain that elementary school girls would necessarily be familiar with this historical figure. (As a matter of fact, it was another queen Mary, namely Mary I (1516–1558), the daughter of Henry VIII and Catherine of Aragon, who was tarnished with the negative label of "Bloody Mary" because of the many bloody persecutions occurring during her reign.) A Freudian rather than a historical gloss on the headless image might construe the loss of a "maiden head" as a symbol of lost virginity, a loss in which the breaking of the hymen could result in blood flowing. The possible erotic connotations of the term "Bloody Mary" are perhaps suggested by the folk term for a well-known drink. A "Bloody Mary" is comprised of tomato juice, Vodka, and a splash of Tabasco Sauce. A "Virgin Mary" is the same concoction minus the Vodka.

More plausible is a hypothetical rationale for the name "Mary Worth." A girl is socialized into believing that her "worth" as a female will be realized through achieving womanhood, marriage, bearing children, etc. To be, then, a worthy Mary, one must first become a woman, hence experience menarche. This, I suspect, is the reason why "Mary Worth" was selected as an alternative name for "Bloody Mary." (The fact that the comic strip character Mary Worth is a post-menopausal widow offering advice to young girls may also be relevant.) In terms of symbol substitution, if we take the two names as synonymous, then "Mary" is the constant, and "Bloody" must be equivalent to "Worth" which is precisely the argument here advanced. (I wonder if "Mary Whales" is a rendering of "Mary wails" with the idea that crying might occur as an emotional response to menarche, especially if young girls are kept in the dark about it, the latter situation perhaps suggested by the "turning out the lights" to set the stage for the ritual.)

The consistent utilization of a mirror in the Bloody Mary ritual confirms Langlois's intuition that the image is in some sense a self-image. (Texts 6 and 10 make this explicit.) Little girls influenced by a host of cultural factors ranging from Barbie Dolls to mass media advertising have already begun to worry about their appearance. "Looking good" to both peers and to members of the opposite sex is surely a desideratum. A mirror is an obvious source of narcissistic pleasure (or concern) in this respect. Curiously, Aristotle is alleged to have said that "if a menstruating woman looks into a mirror, not only is the polish lost, but the person who next looks into the mirror will be bewitched. Pliny, speaking of this tarnishing effect on mirrors, says the polish can be restored by having the same woman look steadily upon the back of the mirror" (Novak 1916:272). Anthropologist Wallace reports that among the Mohave, a girl experiencing menses "must not look at her image in water or in a mirror or she will become cross-eyed' " (1948:37).

With regard to the supposed bewitching effect of menstruating women gazing into mirrors, we recall that the Knapps wondered why the comic strip figure of Mary Worth had become a mirror **witch** (1976:242), a sentiment echoed by Brunvand (1986:82). In a fascinating discussion of the folklore of menstruation, it has been suggested that "in folklore, the conclusion is that menstruation causes a woman to act like a witch" (Delaney, Lupton, and Toth 1977:124). Devereux goes so far as to claim that "The Menstruating Woman as a Witch" is the central theme of the psychoanalytic approach to menstruation (1950:252). The fact that in many versions of the Bloody Mary ritual, the summoned figure menaces the participating girls by attacking them, usually by scratching, resulting in the drawing of blood, would tend to support Devereux's thesis "that all forms of genital bleeding are, unconsciously at least, imagined to be the result of aggression" (1950:251). As to why the Bloody Mary figure might be justified so to speak in attacking prepubescent girls, some reports suggest that it might be a punishment for sins, real or imaginary: "If you've sinned or done anything evil in your life" (text 1) which would seem to offer some support for Karen Horney's suggestion that "the onset of menstruation . . . for the girl who has a fear of being damaged by masturbation, emotionally means a definite proof that this damage has in fact occurred" (Horney 1973:241).

With the aid of the hypothesis that the Bloody Mary ritual is a prepubescent fantasy about the imminent onset of menses, we may now re-read the text reported by Bronner cited above. To summon the ghost, the girls go into the bathroom where they prick their fingers with a pin to draw a drop of blood. The "flowing" of blood from their bodies evidently induces a young pale-faced girl to appear in the mirror with "blood running down her face from a large cut in her forehead" (1988:169). In Freudian terms, this would be an instance of "upwards displacement' with blood issuing from the head instead of from the urinogenital area. This upwards displacement is substantiated not only by the indubitable historical relationship between the words "maidenhood" and "maidenhead," but also by the assignment of facial features to the vagina, e.g., as mouth with lips (labia) which confirms the symbolic equivalence of head and genital area.

We may also return to the problematic text presented by Langlois. The particular coalescence of the Bloody Mary figure with the Vanishing Hitchhiker can now be interpreted. Recall that the Bloody Mary hitchhiker left "a wet spot with blood on the [back] seat". One of the greatest causes of anxiety for young girls newly pubescent is that they may "show' or "spot." Typically, nervous girls repeatedly check the back of their slip, skirt, or dress to see if there are any telltale blood spots. Field research indicates that "menstruation was considered an event to be hidden and girls expressed concern about noticeable staining" (Williams 1980:16). Fears about "showing" are common (Ernster 1977:21). An intriguing feminist argument suggests that menstrual taboos generally are basically imposed by men as part of an overall male chauvinist effort to subjugate women—women bleed because they are inferior beings—and furthermore even women's attempts to conceal their menstruation from men are also attributable ultimately to male, not female esthetics (Laws 1990:128–30, 129).

The fear of leaving a spot of blood (which males might see) might explain the substitution of a wet blood spot in the standard Vanishing Hitchhiker legend in place of the more usual token of scarf, pocketbook, etc. But why did that particular legend combine with the Bloody Mary tradition? To answer this question, we must briefly consider the latent content of the legend.

Brunvand entitled one of his popular anthologies of legends *The Vanishing Hitchhiker* and he provides a substantial number of interesting versions of the legend (1981:24–46), but his attractive subtitle "American Urban Legends & **Their Meanings**" (my emphasis) notwithstanding, one looks in vain for any discussion of the possible meaning(s) of the legends in Brunvand's compilation. Michael Goss in an entire book devoted to the legend, *The Evidence for Phantom Hitch-Hikers*, avers that "the story must have **some** meaning, **some** significance" (1984:30, 32, his emphasis). However, Goss's major concern is that of a parapsychologist intent upon "proving' that ghosts may really exist and that the legend may represent literal history so to speak, not folkloristic fantasy. In his book-length treatment of the legend, Goss can do no more than propose the following vague "theory" of what may "lie behind the allure of the Phantom Hitch-Hiker." According to Goss, "Not sexuality nor car worship, though these may play subsidiary or contributory roles, but a sense of adventure: a timeless adventure, a Romance of the Open Road" (1984:136–37). At least Goss deserves plaudits for realizing that such legends may mean something. But "romance of the open road" does not really address all of the particular details of the legend.

The association of the legend with the Bloody Mary ritual makes it logical to assume that it might possibly have something to do with the transition from girlhood to womanhood. If we see the legend in metaphorical terms, then we can appreciate it as a symbolic morality narrative, a cautionary tale. A girl who hitch-hikes, that is, allows herself to be "picked up" by a perfect (male) stranger, runs the risk of losing her virtue (signaled by the wet blood spot in the car's backseat, a well-known locus of teen-age and even pre-teen necking and petting). The car to prepubescent girls and boys represents a potential mobile bedroom. Souped-up cars used to be called "hot rods," a bit of argot fraught with phallic overtones. Moreover, and this is critical, a girl who allows herself to be picked up in this way can never go home again. In more explicit terms, a girl who has once lost her chastity is punished for all eternity by trying desperately though to no avail to return to the sanctity of home with all its associations of family values. With this reading of the legend, we can see how a "Bloody Mary" ritual in which a girl bridges the transition from prepubescent girl to nubile nymph might be related to a story about the dangerous consequences of a girl's being picked up by a male driver with a hot rod.

I believe that my interpretation of the Bloody Mary ritual (and the Vanishing Hitchhiker legend) is reasonable and that it plausibly takes account of the actual traits of this extremely popular piece of American folklore. But I realize that many conservative literal-minded folklorists as well as informants familiar with Bloody Mary may not agree. I can imagine such informants saying words to the effect: "I participated in it myself and I never once thought about menstruation" or "I know the Vanishing Hitchhiker legend, and I never once thought of it in terms of the incipent danger of a girl's being picked up by a total stranger". Precisely! This is because the majority of folklorists are unable or unwilling to recognize the unconscious content of folklore fantasy. If individuals knew, consciously knew, what they were doing when they participated in symbolic rituals, or told jokes, or sang folksongs, etc. they could not perform such. Folklore as a socially sanctioned outlet to permit individuals to do what is normally not permitted by society, superego, conscience, normative morality, and the like often needs the guise or disguise of fantasy. This is why it is so often taboo topics which inspire the creation and perpetuation of folklore. So the fact that participants in Bloody Mary rituals might not be able to articulate fears about the menarche in no way invalidates the theory proposed in this essay. Quite the contrary. I would not in the least expect most girls from age 7 to 12 to confirm my analysis.

Is the topic of menstruation taboo in American society? As Buckley and Gottlieb note in their useful survey of anthropological research on the subject, "In the West we are accustomed to thinking of menstruation as largely negative. It is 'the curse'..." (1988:32). There is no doubt about it. The plethora of traditional euphemisms—more than one hundred—attests to its taboo status (cf. Joffe 1948, Boone 1954, Larsen 1963, Ernster 1975, Elaney, Lupton and Toth 1977:92–94, Laws 1990:80–982). Some terms are used by men; others by women; a few by both men and women. With regard to folk speech, it is noteworthy that there does seem to be a decided gender distinction in the very pronunciation of the word "menstruation." American men tend to use four syllables in contrast to women who typically use only three in "menstration" without the "u". Most dictionaries (presumably compiled chiefly by men) include only the men's pronunciation.

One could argue that the more folk speech (circumlocutions, euphemisms) for a given item or activity, the more taboo it is likely to be. In the present context, it is surely noteworthy that one of the ninety expressions reported by Joffe in 1948 was one from a woman in the American military: "I'm Bloody Mary today" (1948:183, 185). This constitutes prima facie evidence that "Bloody Mary" can refer to menstruation.

The taboo status of menstruation and the "shame" wrongly associated with its presence means that even in the late twentieth century, little girls are often kept in the dark about it, a metaphor which is apt in the light of the darkness imposed as part of setting the stage for Bloody Mary rituals—which are either performed at night, e.g., midnight, or in bathrooms during the day with the lights turned off. Some parents and teachers, products of repressed American culture, are reluctant to discuss menstruation openly with little girls. As a result, the subject remains mysterious, shrouded in secrecy. It is "scary" but something that every little girl will encounter sooner or later.

According to one study, since "nice women do not discuss such matters," many young girls have little or no prior information about the menarche. One southern white individual "recalled spending the afternoon in an outdoor privy reciting a biblical verse that she had been taught would staunch bleeding" (Snow and Johnson 1977:2737). This latter vignette is reminiscent of one in the 1976 motion picture *Carrie* based upon the 1974 novel by Stephen King, in which early on the innocent main character is shown in a shower in a state of shock, not able to comprehend or understand what has occurred—her first menses! (Carrie's possession of special supernatural powers—often attributed to menstruating women [cf. Devereux 1950:253] and the final dramatic scene at the senior prom when a bucket of blood is unceremoniously dumped on Carrie suggest that the entire plot is basically an extended menstrual fantasy. When in March of 1997, I specifically asked Stephen King about my interpretation of *Carrie*, he would neither confirm nor deny it, saying only that he thought that he drew upon the alleged association between menstruating girls and poltergeist powers, [cf. Houppert 1999:116–21].)

In the absence of reliable detailed information about the whole physiological process of menstruation, little girls turn to folklore for the "facts," just as little boys tend to first learn about sexual activity from "dirty" jokes. The Bloody Mary ritual may not be a scientifically accurate picture of menstruation, but it does represent an anticipatory image of a forthcoming major event in the individual female's life cycle. Just as "dirty" jokes do not necessarily describe sexual activity with unvarnished objectivity so "Bloody Mary" may distort the details of actual menarche. The folklore about an event thus may, and very often does, precede the event in question. So it is that young girls learn one or more of the many euphemisms for menstruation before experiencing it (Ernster 1975:12).

The proposed explanatory rationale underlying the Bloody Mary ritual has the decided advantage of being able to illuminate the myriad details of the ritual. As a prepubescent fantasy about the somewhat fearsome but inevitable onset of menarche, it is enacted usually by an individual girl (or an all-girl group), it takes place in a bathroom, it involves a bloody image, sometimes a bloody self-image appears, and the ritual may conclude with the flushing of a toilet. I would hope that anyone proposing an alternative theory of the Bloody Mary ritual would be able to account for all these various distinctive features.

We can now better understand the aura surrounding the ritual. Little girls admit that they are somewhat apprehensive about participating in the ritual. Some are so frightened that they elect not to do so; others do enter the bathroom but with the sincere hope that the bloody image will not appear. One might legitimately ask why, if the ritual is so "scary," do little girls participate in it at all? I suspect the answer lies in peer pressure. Although it can be an individual activity or performed singly, it is much more often a matter of a small group of girls, three to five in number, huddling together in the dark in a bathroom. The strong desire to be "one of the gang" makes it difficult for a girl to refuse her comrades' request to participate. And, of course, biologically speaking, it is not possible for any girl to refuse to acknowledge the appearance of the menarche when it finally does occur. In some pubescent girl groups, there is even an unspoken competition as to who among them will be the first to reach menarche.

If there is validity in the feminist hypothesis that it is males who have defined menstruation as something "unpleasant" and "disgusting" thereby compelling oppressed women to accept this "male" definition of a female natural bodily function which in turn contributes to feelings of so-called self-hate (Laws 1990:207), then the Bloody Mary ritual may function as a positive rite of passage for young premenarchal girls. Rather than being persuaded by their culture to feel shame and embarrassment about menstruation, the ritual might be construed as an attempt to celebrate the onset of menses.

Let me close as I began. While there will always be an unending demand for the publication of folklore texts—the popular appeal of folklore data is not likely to fade—I believe it is incumbent upon professional folklorists to do more than simply compile anthologies of children's folklore or modern legends. In the final analysis, there should be refined analysis!

Note
1. I wish to thank the following folklore students for their valuable reports of the Bloody Mary ritual: Amanda Feyerabend, Peter Norby, Maria Villavivencio, Deanna Ramsay, Sarah Pulleyblank, Rocio Ferreira, Sheila R. Chung, Courtney Levine, and Moonju Ann Kim among more than fifty others.

References Cited

Ackerman, Robert, 1991. *The Myth and Ritual School*. New York: Garland.
Bennett, Gillian, and Paul Smith. 1993. *Contemporary Legend: A Folklore Bibliography*. New York: Garland.
Boone, Lalia Phipps. 1954. The Vernacular of Menstruation. *American Speech* 29:297–98.
Bronner, Simon J. 1988. *American Children's Folklore*. Little Rock: August House.
Brunvand, Jan Harold. 1981. *The Vanishing Hitchhiker: American Urban Legends & Their Meanings*. New York: W. W. Norton.
———. 1986. *The Mexican Pet*. New York: W. W. Norton.
———. 1993. *The Baby Train & Other Lusty Urban Legends*. New York: W. W. Norton.
Buckley, Thomas, and Alma Gottlieb. 1988. A Critical Appraisal of Theories of Menstrual Symbolism. In *Blood Magic: The Anthropology of Menstruation*. Eds. Thomas Buckley and Alma Gottlieb, pp. 3–50. Berkeley: University of California Press.
Cochran, Robert, and Martha Cochran. 1970. Some Menstrual Folklore of Mississippi. *Mississippi Folklore Register* 4:108–113.
Crawfurd, Raymond. 1915. Notes on the Superstitions of Menstruation. *The Lancet* 189:1331–36.
Dégh, Linda, ed. 1980. *Indiana Folklore: A Reader*. Bloomington: Indiana University Press.
Delaney, Janice, Mary Jane Lupton, and Emily Toth. 1977. *The Curse: A Cultural History of Menstruation*. New York: Mentor.
Devereux, George. 1950. The Psychology of Feminine Genital Bleeding: An Analysis of Mohave Indian Puberty and Menstrual Rites. *International Journal of Psycho-Analysis* 31:237–57.
Ernster, Virginia L. 1975. American Menstrual Expressions. *Sex Roles* 1:3–13.
———. 1977. Expectations About Menstruation Among Premenarcheal Girls. *Medical Anthropology Newsletter* 8(4):16–25.
Goss, Michael. 1984. *The Evidence for Phantom Hitch-Hikers*. Wellingborough: The Aquarian Press.
Grimes, Ronald L. 1985. *Research in Ritual Studies*. Metuchen: Scarecrow Press.
Hiscock, Philip. 1996. Bloody Mary, Bloody Mary, . . . *FOAFtale News* 39:15.
Horn, Maurice. 1977. *Women in the Comics*. New York: Chelsea House.
———. 1996. *100 Years of American Newspaper Comics: An Illustrated Encyclopedia*. New York: Gramercy Books.
Horney, Karen. 1973. *Feminine Psychology*. New York: W. W. Norton.
Houppert, Karen. 1999. *The Curse: Confronting the Last Unmentionable Taboo: Menstruation*. New York: Farrar, Straus and Giroux.
Joffe, Natalie F. 1948. The Vernacular of Menstruation. *Word* 4:181–86.
Knapp, Mary, and Herbert Knapp. 1976. *One Potato, Two Potato . . . : The Secret Education of American Children*. New York: W. W. Norton.
Langlois, Janet. 1978. "Mary Whales, I Believe in You": Myth and Ritual Subdued. *Indiana Folklore* 11:5–33.
Larsen, Virginia L. 1963. Psychological Study of Colloquial Menstrual Expressions. *Northwest Medicine* 62:874–77.
Laws, Sophie. 1990. *Issues of Blood: The Politics of Menstruation*. London: Macmillan.
Malmberg, Denise 1982. "Sorry, I'm Bloody Mary today"—synen pa menstruation i forskning och i folkliga forestallningar. *Tradisjon* 12:59–76.
———. 1991. *Skammens roda blomma? Menstruationen och den menstruerande kvinnan i svensk tradition*. Etnolore 11. Uppsala: Etnologiska institutionen.
Mead, Margaret. 1955. *Male and Female*. New York: Mentor.
Novak, Emil. 1916. The Superstition and Folklore of Menstruation. *Johns Hopkins Hospital Bulletin* 27 (307):270–74.
Segal, Robert A. 1980. The Myth-Ritualist Theory of Religion. *Journal for the Scientific Study of Religion* 19:173–85.

Snow, Loudell F., and Shirley M. Johnson. 1977. Modern Day Menstrual Folklore: Some Clinical Implications. *Journal of the American Medical Association* 237 (25):2736–39.

Vosselmann, Fritz. 1936. *La menstruation: legendes, coutumes, superstitions*. Paris: L'Expansion Scientifique Francaise.

Wallace, William J. 1948. The Girls' Puberty Rite of the Mohave. *Proceedings of the Indiana Academy of Science* 57:37–40.

Williams, Lenore Robinson. 1980. *Beliefs and Attitudes of Young Girls Regarding Menstruation*. M.S. in Nursing thesis, Case Western Reserve University.

6

The Elephant Walk and Other Amazing Hazing

MALE FRATERNITY INITIATION
THROUGH INFANTILIZATION AND FEMINIZATION

(with Lauren Dundes)

The history of hazing is long and filled with cruel practices (Carus 1909, Nuwer 1999:92–115). Hazing is somewhat analogous to what was known in England as "fagging" (Thwing 1878–79:331, Hutchinson 1896), but fagging is more a matter of personal servitude whereas "hazing is a test of loyalty taken by a 'pledge' or prospective member to gain acceptance into a fraternity" (Leslie, Taff, and Mulvihill 1985:53). As defined by Connecticut, one of the thirty-five states that has banned hazing, it is "any action which recklessly or intentionally endangers the health or safety of a person for the purpose of initiation, admission into or affiliation with, or as a condition for continued membership in a student organization" (Lewis 1991:63; for a sampling of additional legal definitions, see the language of several other state antihazing statutes provided by Buchanan et al. 1982).

Hazing is sometimes mistakenly confused with pranks, but pranks, especially college pranks, involve hoaxes and are rarely hurtful (Steinberg 1992:xi). Pranks are usually campuswide public events such as publishing bogus rival college newspapers or kidnapping or painting a notable statue. In contrast, hazing is a private, usually "secret" ritual carried out by an individual fraternity.

Hazing is very much associated with all-male college fraternities—some fraternities are now coed—although it is also found among athletic groups, the military, and businesses. The strength of fraternities varies from campus to campus (Bronner 1990:127, Egan 1985:208), but wherever one finds fraternities, one is likely to find some form of hazing the latest candidates for membership. Of some 168 injuries and deaths caused by hazing from 1923 to 1982, 161 of the victims were male (Leslie, Taff, and Mulvihill 1985:61). In some instances, a shortage of regular dormitory housing may motivate individuals to join fraternities in the hope of finding suitable accommodations and convivial dining facilities (DeParle 1988:40). In other cases, students join fraternities to gain a sense of belonging that often replicates a family environment. By hazing prospective members (pledges) in this surrogate family milieu, members satisfy an unconscious need to bolster their own sense of masculinity as well as to resolve tension resulting from child-rearing practices.

The focus of this essay is on the traditional initiation practices found in American fraternities (and to a much lesser extent, sororities). It is clear that fraternities inasmuch as they involve secrecy and exclusivity are a subset of the larger category of secret societies and fraternal orders. There is a substantial scholarship devoted to secret societies (e.g., Simmel 1906, Webster 1968), but generally speaking, discussions of the larger category tend not to treat college fraternities and their customs in any depth if at all. The same holds for general treatises on puberty rites and initiation rituals (e.g., Young 1965, La Fontaine 1985). Yet fraternity hazing rituals have their own special features that we believe fully merit scholarly consideration.

Young men desiring to join a particular fraternity are subjected to a series of tests that they must successfully pass or survive in order to be ultimately inducted into the all-male group of their choice. These tests are traditional in their sadistic structure and serve the purpose of compelling the fraternity hopefuls to submit to humiliating and in some cases painful punishment. The apparent paradox inherent in these established hazing routines is that in order to prove one's masculinity, one often has to assume a female or feminine role. Inasmuch as this "female" behavior is enacted in front of an all-male audience, it necessarily entails an implication of homosexuality (Larguèze 1995:80). It is our contention that it is precisely the fear of being judged effeminate that underlies many of the humiliating trials inflicted on the newest cohort of fraternity pledges. Living in a single-sex housing unit requires that young men

Fraternity Initiation through Infantilization and Feminization

become accustomed to undressing in front of other young men and perhaps being seen naked in communal shower facilities. Privacy is often at a premium under such conditions, and young men who may have left home for the first time have to get used to sharing close quarters with relative strangers.

Many of the most obscene of these fraternity rituals are not widely known by the general public, and, in some cases, they are supposed to be kept secret from nonmembers of the fraternity, college authorities, and parents. Explicit sexual allusions or miming sexual acts in initiation ceremonies are part of what has been termed "the ritualization of obscenity" (Larguèze 1995:78).

One of the most typical of these rituals is known as the "Elephant Walk." The name is borrowed from a well-known circus act in which elephants parade themselves single file with each elephant using its trunk to grasp the tail of the elephant in front of it. As with all forms of folklore, these initiation rituals exhibit multiple existence and variation. That is, there are different versions of the "Elephant Walk" and no two versions will be absolutely identical. In one fairly tame version, "the pledges, wearing only boxer shorts, are made to crawl in a circle, each with his nose in the preceding pledge's *derriere*" (Egan 1985:63). Another version reported on the UCLA campus in 1976 has naked fraternity pledges walking in a circle, holding the penis of the male directly behind them. The first male to get an erection goes to the center of the circle and the other pledges proceed to masturbate and ejaculate upon him. Here we see several prominent themes of these rituals at work. Young men are not supposed to become sexually aroused by the sight of or contact with the genitals of their fellow fraternity members. Any male who gets an erection when he is among an exclusively male group immediately becomes suspected of harboring homosexual tendencies. Ejaculating on him feminizes him inasmuch as he is forced to accept the semen of his betters.

Another version of the "Elephant Walk," this time from the Berkeley campus in 1991, has the pledges take off their clothing and get in a circle, with each individual facing the back of another. They then bend over, and put one thumb in their mouth and the other thumb in the person's rear in front of them. They then proceed to walk in a circle, keeping their thumb in the rear end of the person in front of them. If, during the walk, any of their thumbs fall out of their comrades' rear ends, they must switch thumbs such that the thumb that was previously in a rear end must be put into their mouth. The walk continues until the person in charge lets them stop. In Canada, seven rookie members of a male hockey team "refused to conduct the 'Elephant Walk' around a veteran player's home," with the Elephant Walk described as "all of the rookies stripping naked and slowly walking in a line in public while each rookie is holding the penis of the individual behind him" (Bryshun 1997:898, 94n6).

We know that the Elephant Walk goes back at least to 1931. In that year Ross Lockridge Jr. pledged Phi Gamma Delta at Indiana University. He recollected a hazing ritual called the "Elephant Drill." The pledges "were stripped naked and ordered to follow one another on all fours, goosing one another and then sucking fingers" (Lockridge 1994:98).

Lest the reader think that this kind of behavior is a rare occurrence, we may mention a hazing ritual called the "Dog Lick." At the University of Southern California circa 1990 this consisted of a line of naked pledges ordered "to get down on all fours" and to lick the naked posterior of the individual directly in front of them. One participant in this ritual recalled "I couldn't see my other pledge brothers performing the 'dog lick,' but as soon as I felt a warm, hard tongue swipe through the crack of my butt, I knew I would really have to do it! I don't know how, but I licked my pledge brother's hairy butt. It was so sick! I can't comprehend why I did the things I did just to get into my fraternity" (Wright 1996:13).

It is difficult to obtain eyewitness accounts of such rituals as the Elephant Walk because informants would almost certainly be reluctant to admit that they themselves had participated in these events. Also fraternities usually require their initiated members to swear that they will never reveal any of the fraternity's secret handshakes, oaths, or rituals. This appears to be a general characteristic of secret societies. Gist observes, "The most conspicuous aspect of the ritualistic obligation . . . is the formal promise to keep inviolate the secrets of the order . . . the obligation ordinarily states specifically the conditions of secrecy: the candidate must not write, print or impart verbally any of the secrets relating to passwords, ritual, or other secret features. These are the supreme taboos of secret fraternalism" (1940:93, cf. Leemon 1972:136). For this reason, students rarely report hazing to authorities (Nuwer 1999:42–43).

Fraternity Initiation through Infantilization and Feminization   99

Sometimes, hazing events exist in the form of legends, and it is not always clear whether such legends are based on actual historical reality. (For a discussion of fraternity initiation legends that often end with the unanticipated death of a pledge, see Bronner 1990:162–65.)

The following is a legend reported on the Berkeley campus dating from April of 1994. Whether the incident actually occurred is uncertain.

> There's this one where there is a bunch of guys, and each guy gets a bunch of M and M's, and they have to take off all their clothes and shove the M and M's up their butts. Right? And the one that who, like, can't hold the M and M's or that can hold the least M and M's . . . Hmm . . . and they take one guy . . . what do they do? . . . O.K., they take the guy who can hold the least M and M's and the guy who holds the most M and M's (he's already butt naked), and they pour beer down his back really slowly so that it clings to his body and it has to go down his butt crack and the guy who can hold the least M and M's has to sit and drink the beer.

This legend, whether or not it reflects an actual hazing event, displays some of the same themes already mentioned. The individual who "can't take it" in the rear is punished by having to drink a fluid, that is, beer, which has been in contact with the rear end of an individual who has proven that he can take it. While it may not be pleasant for that individual to have beer poured down his back and backside, the real humiliation clearly belongs to the poor soul who has to drink the beer.

One of the most curious forms of symbolic emasculation involves a spin-off from the "Circle Jerk." In the true Circle Jerk, adolescent boys simply masturbate together, sometimes betting as to who will ejaculate first (Legman 1975:111). In a typical variant, initiates in a circle are required to fondle the genitals of the man sitting next to them until that individual has an orgasm. But in this spin-off ritual, initiates are told that they are to participate in a "Circle Jerk." The rules, however, turn out to be different. In a three-minute time period, each individual must pull as much hair as possible from the man to his right's left leg. At the same time that he is pulling hair from the leg to his right, the hair from his own left leg is being pulled out by the individual immediately to his left. After three minutes, the initiates are told to get up and an attempt is made to determine who has collected the smallest ball of hair. Once this person is identified, all of the hair pulled from all the initiates is collected and rolled into one ball, and the loser is told he must swallow it. In versions from Berkeley in 1969, just as the loser prepares to do this and the hair ball reaches his lips or is just inside his mouth, he is stopped by the person in charge. He is then ridiculed for following such an irrational order (although he would have suffered even more ridicule had he refused to obey).

This ritual involves the symbolic nature of hair, a subject that has inspired considerable debate. The sexual symbolism of hair cannot be denied. No doubt one reason for the symbolism is that it is precisely the appearance of pubic hair that marks sexual maturation among both males and females. In this case, the male initiates are feminized by having to participate in a depilatory ritual. It is girls and women who often make a fetish of removing hair from their legs (as well as underarms and faces). Except for shaving their faces, men make no effort to remove such body hair. The initial masturbatory element of the Circle Jerk is not completely absent as hair and semen can be symbolic equivalents. A common superstition among adolescent males is that if one masturbates, it will inevitably produce hair on one's palm. This is frequently used as a "catch" among junior high school males. One boy will say to another, "Did you know . . . ?" And the dupe almost always glances at his hand to see if there is any telltale hair growing there. Of course, it is semen that gets on the palm as a result of male masturbation, not hair, but the superstition equates semen and hair. In the ritual described above, it is the semen-hair on the leg that is manipulated into a ball to be swallowed by the loser. The loser is thus being forced to ingest the combined masculine products of the group. In a less symbolic version of this at one mid-Atlantic college fraternity (1999), initiates must consume a slice of pizza that has been ejaculated on by members.

Despite the longevity of hazing traditions, there has been relatively little theorizing about their significance. Lionel Tiger in one chapter of his *Men in Groups,* entitled "Men Court Men: Initiations and Secret Societies" (1984:126–55) suggests that the basic function of secret society behavior is to promote "male bonding" (130). This represents the conventional wisdom about hazing. "The humiliations of hazing are said to build bonds, forge a collective identity" (DeParle 1988:45). There is some validity to this view, but there is much more that can be said about the underlying rationale of hazing. Ray Raphael in his book-length study of male initiation rituals in America, *The Men from the Boys*, astutely observes that "the function of hazing ... is to provide a threat of potential failure while simultaneously insisting that the novitiate must actually succeed" (1988:13). Stephen Sweet, in his attempt to apply symbolic interactionist theory to hazing, states that "fraternity initiation rites are designed to terminate or curtail many of the associations that pledges previously held outside of that organization" (1999:359). This is certainly true, but it says little about the specifics of the hazing imposed upon pledges. The same criticism applies to the legitimate attempts to apply Arnold van Gennep's classic 1909 tripartite rites-of-passage schema: separation, transition, and reincorporation to hazing (Leemon 1972, Larguèze 1995:77, Nuwer 1999:55). The pattern is certainly visible in hazing rites, but the mere identification of the pattern does not fully explain the subtle nuances of the hazing practices. Hank Nuwer's valuable books on hazing, *Broken Pledges* (1990), *Wrongs of Passage* (1999), and *High School Hazing* (2000), are thorough documentations of the many tragic deaths caused by fraternity and sorority binge drinking and hazing practices, but he does not attempt to analyze the possible significance of the content of hazing rituals. Perhaps it is the undeniable grossness of some of the details of these rituals that has discouraged scholars from giving them the attention they merit.

In his brief discussion of initiation rituals in North American fraternities, Tiger does note that "the initiations themselves frequently involve partial or complete nudity of initiates, and in many there are homoerotic implications of greater or lesser clarity" (1984:148). Others have made similar comments: "Apparently, there are often rather strong homoerotic overtones in hazing activities" (Ramzy and Bryant 1962:358). Gist in his 1940 survey of fraternal societies in general (not just college fraternities) also remarked that "in some fraternities, the candidate is stripped of his street apparel and made to wear some scanty attire, either his underclothes or some special garment provided by the group" (85). In one survey, nudity along with "dropping food into mouth," "eating unpalatable foods," "paddle swats," and "forced drinking of alcohol" were deemed to be typical hazing activities (Baier and Williams 1983:301). Presumably, the naked state is to symbolize the stripping away of a previous identity as well as representing rebirth—one comes into the world

102 Fraternity Initiation through Infantilization and Feminization

naked, after all, and a readiness to assume a spanking new identity. The insistence that the initiate be naked or in some instances forced to wear a diaper suggests that one important component of fraternity initiation is infantilization.

The importance of infantilization in hazing practices has not been sufficiently recognized. However, Ramzy and Bryant do claim that "it is also possible that the older members, identifying themselves with the new victims, receive infantile gratification from the immature, infantile acts which the newcomers are forced to perform while at the same time they are permitted to seem more mature" (1962:358). And anthropologist Sanday does comment that the fact that pledges are forced to wear diapers is a sign of "their status as infants" (1990:159). One must keep in mind that the initiates are only a year or so younger than the youngest of the members of the fraternity. By infantilizing the recruits, the other members of the fraternity increase the age distance between themselves and the novices. In effect, they become "older" by comparison, simulating the role of parents or parent surrogates. The word "fraternity" comes from the Latin word *frater*, meaning brother. This means that the members of a fraternity are likened to siblings in a family. It may also be relevant that fraternities are on college campuses where there are authority figures like parents, such as professors, deans, and other administration officers. So the members of a fraternity are students who are subject to the whims and unpleasant discipline of college authority much as children are governed by parents who sometimes seem to make unreasonable demands and impose capricious punishments. Hazing allows these fraternity students to displace their own frustration as young adults anxious to liberate themselves from the bonds of parental and now collegiate authority by subjugating a new crop of younger students who wish to join the fraternity. Just as young children may resent the appearance of a new baby and express hostility toward it, so fraternity brothers, despite wanting to recruit new members to their fold, act out their resentment at being displaced by younger "baby" recruits.

A common fraternity initiation practice, paddling (Baier and Williams 1983), often on a bare behind, infantilizes pledges by replicating spanking, a commons means of parental punishment. In some fraternities, when a pledge does something wrong, he receives a "black mark," which leads to a bare-bottomed spanking for each infraction. In other fraternities, a severe paddling is part of the initiation. On some campuses, the paddles, or a representative paddle, are burned in the fraternity house fireplace following the ritual spanking (Olmert 1983:152), perhaps suggesting that the neophytes' period of symbolic infantilization is at an end. Paddling is also an echo of the obstetrician spanking the newborn as s/he enters the world. In this manner, paddling serves as a type of rebirth into an identity as a fraternity brother.

Other common fraternity practices include dropping food into the mouth and forced drinking of alcohol (Baier and Williams 1983). Both of these activities simulate a parent feeding an infant. Infants, who cannot feed themselves, have food and drink inserted into their mouths, by parents who often must guess at when their baby needs sustenance. The fact that the food given to pledges is often unpalatable (Baier and Williams 1983) is certainly reminiscent of childhood, wherein parents force their infants and children to eat foods of an unfamiliar type characterized by a strange texture or unpleasant flavor, from the child's point of view. The offensive taste and texture makes the forced consumption of raw eggs a common fraternity hazing practice. In a variation of this practice reported at Berkeley from the 1960s to the 1990s and at the University of Southern California (Wright 1996:14) that combines the forced insertion of food into the mouth with food that is highly repugnant, pledges must sometimes pass a raw egg mouth to mouth, like a kiss, without breaking the yolk. Here is an account of this ritual at the University of Southern California: "The Hell Master often cracked a raw egg over the head of the first pledge and poured the yolk into the pledge's mouth. The pledge was then commanded to pass the yolk mouth to mouth to the next kneeling pledge, and so on down the line of twenty or so pledges. If the yolk broke, the pledge receiving it had to swallow it, and a new yolk had to be passed from the beginning. Pledges were forced to pass a cube of butter in the same way" (Wright 1996:14).

When infants are fed or are just beginning to learn to feed themselves, they frequently make quite a mess such that some of the food is inevitably smeared on their faces, hands, and on their clothing. Bibs catch some of the overflow, but not all of it. In a fraternity punishment at a mid-Atlantic university in 1963, the pledges were obliged to eat "square meals" during Greek Week. According to Leemon, " 'Square meals' referred to lifting one's fork straight up from the plate to the level of the mouth, and then bringing the fork to the mouth in a straight line from its prior position. Food frequently dropped from the pledges' forks to their laps or on the front of their sacks [that they were required to wear]" (1972:167).

This might explain part of the pleasure in subjecting pledges to a shower of a vast array of disgusting food mixtures. For example, at Duke University in 1979, "Unhappy solutions of egg yolks, vaseline, and month-old yogurt would be freely applied" (DeParle 1988:40). At the University of Texas in the 1950s, one ex-fraternity member remembers being pelted with "a relentless stream of eggs" covering him "with the oozing yellow yolk, which stuck against the molasses and chicken feed and castor oil in a great soggy mess" (Morris 1967:157). Sometimes the pledges were asked to ingest such unappetizing mixtures. Leemon describes one such incident at the mid-Atlantic university that he studied: "In the middle of the kitchen floor were two candles, between which was a large kettle that contained a mixture of raw eggs, salt, pepper, mustard, corn flakes, maple-flavored syrup, catsup, and vinegar" (1972:183). The pledge was then ordered to kneel in front of the candles and kettle and take a mouthful of the brew. He sucked some of the mixture into his mouth without the aid of utensils and some of it inevitably got "smeared on the pledge's nose and chin" (1972:184). It is not uncommon for pledges to vomit after being compelled to eat or drink some unpleasant concoction, and this could possibly replicate infant regurgitation. Incidentally, the regressive behavior involved in "food fights," which occur on occasion in college dining areas is also very likely an expression of infantilization. Infants typically express their frustration and anger by dropping food on the floor or throwing it at their caretakers.

Another common practice, dumping water on unsuspecting pledges, is like a bath, an activity imposed upon young children at the apparent pleasure of the parents.

In the case of "Mattress Toast" (reported at University of California, Berkeley, 1983), an old mattress is urinated on by all the members of the fraternity. The pledges must lie down on the mattress on their backs and make a toast regarding the reason they wish to join the fraternity, after which a member pours a shot of hard liquor into their mouths. So in this case, an infantilized pledge is lying in a bed that has been wet (an inevitable occurrence in infancy) and then forced to drink—not by his own hand, but by that of a member. The bed-wetting simulation is yet another example of enforced infantilization, in this case, alluding to the painful process of toilet training. This would also help to explain why some hazing rituals including submerging the pledges in "vats of filth" (Sweet 1999:357). Some of the hazing rituals reported are more explicit with respect to references to toilets. For example, a report from a Berkeley student in 1971 claimed that a person being initiated was forced to have his head put in a urinal that contained fresh urine and have it flushed. This practice was known as the "Dirty Swirl." The same informant indicated that he knew a milder version practiced at Maryknoll Junior Seminary (high school) in Mountain View, California, in 1964, where a toilet bowl was used instead of a urinal and it contained clean water. There are also versions of the mattress ritual where water rather than urine is used. The pledges are told to kneel on a mattress in the backyard of the fraternity house and surprised by buckets of water poured on them from above, a technique also used when the pledges are told to pose for a group photograph (Leemon 1972:178).

Practices reported at Indiana University in 1931 confirm the emphasis on toilet behavior. Pledges "were blindfolded and made to eat peanut-covered bananas floating in johns, and were for routine defecation forced to sit on the john backward" (Lockridge 1994:98). At Berkeley in 1962, Colton describes a similar ritual whereby blindfolded pledges were forced to eat bananas taken from toilets and to drink vinegar from a squeeze bottle after being told to "Drink a brother's piss" (1993:48). In Sanday's version, the banana is placed in a toilet that had been lined with a plastic bag (1990:169). In another report, the soggy bananas are floating in a solution of peanut butter and water in a plastic-lined toilet bowl (Egan 1985:66). In Canada, blindfolded drunken rookie athletes were forced to bob for applies in toilets they were led to believe contained feces (O'Hara 2000:51). In 1981, hazing rituals at a fraternity at the State University of New York's Old Westbury campus included forcing pledges to eat dog food (cf. Lewis 1991:63) and also to drink a mixture of oil and water as a laxative, thus forcing them to defecate.

A hazing ritual known as a "Candy Ass Trial" may also serve to illustrate the toilet training infantilization theme. If a male pledge appears to give undue attention to a particular female—for example, if he gives a girl flowers—he may be subject to a Candy Ass Trial. According to a report from a Berkeley student in 1970, the Delta Upsilon fraternity held mock trials usually once a year. After a day devoted to drinking, the brothers strip the accused and place a sticky substance of some kind (honey, syrup, peanut butter) on his buttocks after which cornflakes or flour are applied to the same area. The defendant is then put naked inside a sleeping bag and deposited on the doorstep of the sorority in which the girl in question resides. The girl's house has been informed ahead of time so that all the residents are hanging out of windows watching. The victim's problem is getting back to the Delta Upsilon. The sleeping bag is arranged in such a way that he cannot get out of it without exposing himself and it is impossible to hop while in it. Sometimes the girl takes pity on him and brings him a towel that he can use to cover himself. The idea that someone is caught sleeping with his posterior covered with a disgusting sticky substance surely has suggestions of a small child who has had an "accident" in bed.

A rather overt illustration of infantilization is a hazing incident involving a female soccer team at the University of Oklahoma. According to a report in the November 1, 1999, issue of *Sports Illustrated,* Kathleen Peay filed a lawsuit against her coach, Bettina Fletcher, charging her with "physical and emotional abuse." On a road trip to the University of New Mexico, the freshmen women were in one van and the upperclassmen in another. Stopping at an elementary school playground—the site may not be insignificant—the freshmen were ordered out of their van and forced to put on adult diapers. Thereupon, Coach Fletcher allegedly produced a banana and insisted that Peay and another player simulate oral sex on it. (For a comparable initiation ritual at the University of Southern California in which women pledges were given a banana and told to suck on the banana in front of fraternity members, see Wright 1996:40.) Players were also photographed with pickles in their mouths. This form of hazing is similar to male hazing in that the victims had to submit to sexual aggression, but unlike the male situation, it is women (doing the hazing) who function as dominant males. So in male hazing, the initiates may be forced to act like women whereas in female hazing, the dominators are women acting like men.

Another example of infantilization in female hazing is reported in a study of public high school sorority initiations. The pledges were required to bring "catsup, eggs, garlic salt, chocolate syrup, shaving cream,

Fraternity Initiation through Infantilization and Feminization 107

and the like" to a park where difficult-to-remove substances were smeared on them, especially on their hair, by senior members of the sorority. The objective was to make the initiate "feel dirty, messy, and ugly." But the most significant detail for the present discussion is that "while the treatment is going on, the pledges are made to play in the sand or on the slides" (Schwartz and Merten 1968:1127). Playing in the sand is an activity clearly linked to very small children, and, for that matter, Ferenczi (1956) has suggested that playing with sand is a sublimated form of playing with feces as part of an evolutionary process in childhood moving gradually from wet substances such as mud (pies) to drier ones such as sand, clay, and Play-Doh. Those skeptical about Ferenczi's suggestion should take account of the fact that pledges are quite often doused with mixtures containing actual excrement (Nuwer 2000:33, 39, 53). For example, in 1992, a Lodi, New Jersey, high school football player had "feces and peanut butter" spread all over his body during his initiation (Nuwer 2000:74).

In discussions of hazing, with few exceptions (Larguèze 1995:80), the subject of sexual inversion seems to have been overlooked. Neither Tiger nor Gist, for example, appear to be aware that in some of the college initiation rituals the male pledges are made to wear women's apparel (Egan 1985:49) or apply women's cosmetics, for example, toenail or fingernail polish.

A graphic example of this is provided by an incident that occurred at the University of Vermont in 1999. According to an account in the *Burlington Free Press* for Sunday, December 12, 1999, the University of Vermont's hockey team held a "big night" rookie initiation party on October 1, where freshman were subjected to traditional hazing, including the Elephant Walk. According to former player Corey LaTulippe, who brought formal charges against the university, he was required to parade around in women's underwear, in addition to suffering other humiliations. Allegedly, he and other freshmen had been instructed to solicit thong underwear from female freshmen at UV. Then, on the night of the party, the freshman members of the team were transported to a "hockey house" wearing female thong underwear and togas. Their fingernails and toenails were painted and their pubic hair shaved.

At Duke University in 1979, a group of pledges finally turned on one of their tormentors. In a form of rebellion known as a "pledge sneak"

(Nuwer 1999:52), they kidnapped him and took him to a motel room, where they sealed his mouth with duct tape. They then stuffed him into a pair of red panties and "other lacy frills" that had been purchased at K-Mart. "That was his only cover when he was deposited that evening, lipsticked, at a sorority formal" (DeParle 1988:46).

A report from a male Berkeley student in 1983 described a pledge ritual that took place in January of 1980. In this ritual, the informant and his fellow pledges were forced to form a line and told that they were now the Radio City Rockettes and that they had to kick in unison, wave their hands above their heads, and turn in circles. Making young men perform as a line of dancing girls, kicking in perfect synchrony, is surely an example of coercive feminization. In Canada, rookie members of a men's basketball team had to dress as women, put on makeup, and then go to school (Bryshun 1997:76).

An additional manifestation of feminization is reflected in some fraternity brothers' application of the word "bitch" to pledges who must act as their personal servants. The use of this term serves to reinforce the pledges' feminization and humiliation. One Berkeley fraternity brother (1995) explains: "I have a few people that are always my bitches. When I see them, I'll say, 'What's up, bitch,' even if I don't want a favor from them." The pledges' compliance with any brother's requests—often chores—replicates the antiquated husband-wife relationship in which traditionally women promised to "obey" their husbands as stipulated in their marriage vows. The word "bitch," denoting a *female* dog, is a term also commonly used in prisons when one male inmate subjugates another, who often is forced to serve as a surrogate woman, both in physical appearance and behavior, which includes chores and sexual favors. The feminizing inherent in using the term "bitch" is reiterated by a student at UC Berkeley (1980) who described the role of such pledges as being "like a maid"—thereby signifying either a girl or a female servant. Another Berkeley student (1995) was more explicit when describing the appellation bitch: "When a fraternity member accepts a role of subservience, he is acting like some meek woman."

A fraternity drinking game ritual called "Whale Tales" (Rhoads 1995:306–7), presumably observed at Michigan State University, features a story told serially by ten brothers who have code names. The initial storyteller signals the one to continue the narrative by mentioning the

Fraternity Initiation through Infantilization and Feminization   109

appropriate code word or nickname. If a brother fails to hear the signal or fails to continue the story immediately, he must chug-a-lug a full glass of beer. At some point, the storyteller stops and the brothers point with their elbows at one particular brother who protests that the proper signal was not given and he refuses to drink. Thereupon, all the brothers except for the accused "stand up around the table and mockingly grasp their shirts with both hands, chest high, with their pointer fingers and thumbs, and pull them in an outward direction to signify imaginary breasts." Then they sing a song directed at the apparent transgressor, the words of which consist essentially of the phrase "You're a woman." Rhoads contends that the ritual promotes a hostile representation of women, for instance, as passive victims, fostering the oppression "of both women and gay men" (1995:307). He fails to comment on the possible symbolic significance of men acting like women (by pretending to have breasts). After all, men could perfectly well demean women without acting out female body parts!

In another instance of feminization called "Spot the Pussy," a variant of musical chairs reported at UC Berkeley in 1969, initiates must run up flights of stairs in time to claim a Coke bottle where there are fewer bottles than pledges. Initiates who return without a bottle are designated "pussies," after which they are ridiculed and punished by having to perform demanding physical exercises. The symbolism is transparent: the pledge without a phallic bottle (not a can) is feminized by a slang term commonly used to refer to female genitals. Calling pledges "pussies" is fairly common (DeParle 1988:46, Colton 1993:41, Sanday 1990:156, 161, 165).

Initiates are also feminized by being awarded the "on the rag" prize given to the member of the fraternity who complained the most during the past year, this according to a Berkeley student in 1983. The penalty for breaching the facade of the stoic male is to be characterized as a menstruating female. The initiation game "Eat the Rag" also uses menstruation to debase pledges (UC Berkeley, 1969). Pledges line up before a long strand of toilet paper covered with catsup and raw eggs. Without the use of their hands, they must then race to stuff the paper and its contents into their mouths (a messy process resulting in food-smeared faces consistent with infantilization). The slowest participants are taunted and forced to perform physical exercise. However, perhaps the most telling instance of menstrual imagery found in male hazing ritual was a detail of the Berkeley Pi Kappa Alpha fraternity's tradition in the early 1960s wherein pledges were obliged to wear a Kotex pad in their crotches while undergoing such ordeals as drinking a "goat shake" consisting of "molasses, vinegar, Worcestershire sauce, mustard, coffee, and prune juice" (Colton 1993:44). Wearing a Kotex pad would constitute a virtual literalization of the "on the rag" metaphor.

Some scholars, especially feminists, who have studied fraternities have emphasized the antiwomen aspects of hazing rituals (Sanday 1990, Sweet 1999:360). And it is certainly true that fraternity values tend to dehumanize and denigrate women and to treat all females as potential sex objects. Fraternity group or gang rapes are a shameful reality as has been well documented (Sanday 1990, Hirsch 1990, Wright 1996:49–62). But as the female director of the Sexual Assault Recovery Services at the University of Florida insightfully remarked, "Men rape for other men" (Hirsch 1990:54). In "gang bangs," initiates must perform in front of their male peers, and "if a man in the room didn't participate, his sexual capacity could be called into question" (54). Interestingly enough, group rape has been interpreted as being essentially homoerotic: "In the 'gang-shag' the relationship of the men to each other is almost openly homosexual, and involving contact with each other's semen; and is much closer than the relation to the woman" (Legman 1968:497). In this analysis, "the gang-shag is a disguised homosexual activity, with the woman simply used as a pretext or coupling-joint" (499). Anthropologist Sanday in her analysis of seriatim sexual intercourse known colloquially as "pulling train" concurs: "By sharing the same sexual object, the brothers are having sex with each other as well" (1990:110). This would seem to confirm Kimmel's observation that "American men define their masculinity, not as much in relation to women, but in relation to each other. Masculinity is largely a homosocial enactment" (1996:7)

It is our contention that most of the scholars studying hazing have failed to appreciate fully the significance of the male initiates having to function as females in the fraternity context. Adolescent males feel a compulsion to break away from the world of women, from the influence of their mothers and precollege teachers, many of whom were female. The repudiation of any trace of female behavior is critical for boys who wish to become full-fledged men (Chodorow 1979:181, Sanday 1990:14, 171). Even at an early age, no boy wants to be known as a "sissy" (the

Fraternity Initiation through Infantilization and Feminization

term coming from "sister"). Kimmel calls this fear of feminization "the specter of the sissy" (1996:122) and claims that men are terrified by the prospect of being labeled as such. The antifemale push becomes a crescendo for high school- and college-age males in the United States. This fear of being feminine or being accused of being feminine is demonstrated in the recounting of antifemale jokes or in publicly displaying antifemale behavior, for instance, treating women as mere sex objects. To be sure, girls and women feel, with some justification, victimized by these covert and overt acts of misogyny, but the basic problem is one of young males unsure about their own masculinity, hence the term "cocky pledge" used to show admiration for a spirited pledge (UC Berkeley, 1979).

Just as fraternity members infantilize newcomers in order to feel older, so the newcomers are feminized to make the fraternity members feel more masculine. Moreover, when the initiates who have withstood the horrors of hazing become themselves members of the fraternity, they are often the first to lead the hazing attack on the next set of incoming pledges. As hazing authority Nuwer notes, "Just as abused children often become abusers, the hazed become the hazers" (1990:55). "Basically, it's the goddamn sophomores who went through it the previous year who want to get even, so they make it worse" (270). This is evidently quite a long-standing tradition. In a compendium of college customs and slang, first published in 1851, hazing is mentioned as a term used at Harvard "to express the treatment which Freshmen sometimes receive from the higher classes, and especially from the Sophomores" (Hall 1968:251). Numerous rules for "Freshman Servitude" are included, such as mandating the running of errands for seniors (Hall 1968:213–25). Writing in 1879 about Harvard and Yale among other institutions, Thwing comments, "The hazing of one year is the mother of the hazing of the next. Every Freshman who is hazed can heal his injured honor only by hazing. So custom perpetuates the evil through successive classes" (1879:333).

The labeling of pledges as "girls" is often quite explicit in fraternity hazing. In one of the few detailed ethnographic investigations of college fraternity life, we're told that the senior member of the fraternity in charge of the pledges ordered them to perform twenty push-ups, after which he said to them, "On your feet, girls" (Leemon 1972:152). Soon thereafter another fraternity member, using a mocking "feminine tone of voice," shouted, "What are you? Girls?" (1972:153). Then the first sen-

Fraternity Initiation through Infantilization and Feminization

ior member dressed down the pledges in a harangue that included "When are you going to show us something? You're always shuffling around the house like girls. You haven't improved at all" (1972:154). On another occasion, the same member reproved the pledges after fifteen push-ups, "You guys are dropping out like flies. What do you think this is, a girl scout camp?" (Leemon 1972:120). The ethnographer in this case makes no comment whatsoever on the use of the repeated reference to "girls". Yet demeaning male pledges by calling them "girls" continues to be standard practice in fraternity initiations (Sanday 1990:159, 165, 167).

The labeling of incoming potential members of a male group in female terms is by no means confined to campus fraternities. In the military, we find a similar phenomenon in basic training institutions, typically called "boot camp." In an autobiographical essay describing details observed while undergoing Marine Corps basic training, Eisenhart noted that "the primary lesson of boot camp towards which all behavior was shaped was to seek dominance" (1975: 16). Any recruit who did not display sufficient aggressive behavior was singled out for abuse by the drill instructor, who called such an individual "girl" or "faggot." In one brutal incident, the DI chastised several men who carried an exhausted comrade during a grueling run: "No goddamn bunch of little girl faggots who can't run seven miles as a unit will get a rest"; then turning to the recruit who was carried, he said, "You're a weak no-good-for-nothing queer." He continued by addressing the whole platoon: "As long as there are faggots in this outfit who can't hack it, you're all going to suffer ... Unless you women get with the program, straighten out the queers, and grow some balls of your own, you best give your soul to God because your ass is mine and so is your mother's on visiting day" (1975:17). The themes are familiar. Recruits who don't measure up are called "girls" or "faggots." The super-macho drill instructor claims to own the recruits' asses (implying they would have to assume the passive homosexual "female" position in an act of sodomy). He even threatens to engage in a sexual act with the recruits' mothers, a final insult to the recruits' masculinity and honor.

Precisely the same technique is found among male athletic groups. An ex-professional football player recalls, "From grade school on, the curse words on the football field are about behaving like a girl. If you don't run fast enough or block or tackle hard enough you're a pussy, a cunt, a sissy" (Kopay and Young 1977:50–51). A Berkeley student told us that he remembered very distinctly his 1991 high school football coach in Darien, Connecticut, would say at the outset of a game, "On the field, *men*," but if the team was losing at the end of the first half, the same coach would say, "Into the locker room, *ladies*." A comparable example can be found in basketball. According to one report, controversial Indiana University basketball coach Bobby Knight "puts sanitary napkins in the lockers of his players to shame them as wusses and make them play more aggressively" (Kimmel 1996:298). A study of hazing in French and Belgian schools noted that boys were forced to wear necklaces made of tampons drenched in red paint (Larguèze 1995:80). This suggests that the pattern we are describing for college fraternities is by no means limited to the United States or, for that matter, to the campus community. Rather it is part of a larger cultural pattern manifested in other male groups, including in the military and in sports. In professional baseball, for instance, St. Louis Cardinals rookies were evidently obliged to "dress up in female wigs and dresses" (Nuwer 2000:66).

One of the most blatant means to feminize a pledge is to have the initiate symbolically enact the passive position of homosexual sodomy. This is achieved by various means, including the anal insertion of fingers, pencils, plastic bottles, and broomstick handles (Vargas 2000). In one reported ritual, "naked pledges have been forced to grip carrots in their teeth and ceremonially dip them into the anuses of brothers lying on their stomachs" (Merton 1985:64). Another more common technique involves the anal insertion of some object such as a hot dog in front of members of the fraternity. In one version reported from a campus in the mid-Atlantic region in 1999, pledges removed a partially inserted hot dog with their teeth. In another version at UC Berkeley (1990), a pledge extruded a hot dog from his sour cream-covered buttocks in order to win a "grosser than gross" rounds contest, only to be outdone by another pledge who picked up the ejected hotdog and bit off the end. It takes very little imagination to recognize that the hot dog symbolizes a phallus and that the sour cream represents semen. A different hazing ritual involving the same element required freshmen to eat numerous "raw hot dogs dredged in tobacco" which usually caused severe nausea (Matthews 1997:88).

Another example of a hazing ritual involving the buttocks is the

114   Fraternity Initiation through Infantilization and Feminization

marshmallow relay race reported at Berkeley in 1962. A pledge had to wait "for a teammate with a marshmallow wedged up his ass to waddle across the room and deposit it for the next leg of the race" while a senior member of the fraternity threatened the pledges with words such as "Losing team eats the marshmallows" (Colton 1993:45). In 1988, a sophomore athlete at Medford High School in Massachusetts reported that he had been compelled to participate in a race with cookies inserted in his buttocks' cheeks where the "losers were forced to eat the cookies at the completion of the perverse race" (Nuwer 2000:71–72).

In 1996, freshman members of the University of Vermont hockey team were made to participate in an event called the "Olive Run" in which they had to "carry olives between their buttocks while being struck with wooden cooking spoons" (O'Hara 2000:52). This use of olives is evidently traditional. "To be initiated to Sigma Chi, Michigan State, 1963, you were required to pick up a stuffed olive off the chapter-room floor using nothing but the naked cheeks of your behind; and, while many "actives" watched and cheered, deliver the olive to a small waiting Dixie Cup" (Ford 1986:234). In a fascinating master's thesis on hazing in sports, based on interviews with thirty athletes from western Canada, one informant provided the following graphic details of a relay race run by rookie football players: "The rookies had to go buck [naked] and we had olive races between the rookies. There's a chunk of ice at one end of the field and you have a bunch of olives sitting on top of it. Rookies have to sit down and pick one up with their ass and run across [the field] and put it down on the other side. You can't touch the olives with your hands or else you have to start again. The first one to move three olives wins the race. The problem is that the ice is so damn cold on your ass, it is really hard to pick them up. Making them stay in your ass while you're running is another thing" (Bryshun 1997:83). In one version of the Olive Run, each runner must squat over a martini glass and drop the ice-cold olive into it. If the pledge misses the glass, he has to eat the olive and start over (Egan 1985:64). Another Canadian relay race involved "rookies running against one another down a hallway, while they had pickles inserted into their (clothed) buttocks. The overall loser of the races was punished by having to eat their own pickle" (Bryshun 1997:65).

Some may hesitate to consider sour cream and marshmallows as possible symbols of semen in these male hazing rituals, but then there is the traditional use of raw egg white to take into account. Uncooked eggs seem to be a fairly common element in hazing ritual. A detail reported by Leemon is quite revealing. In this 1963 incident, the pledges were required to wear a burlap sack and carry various items (a dollar's worth of change, gum, matches, cigarettes, and one raw egg) "at all times in a nylon stocking" (1972:149). When asked by a senior fraternity member for change, cigarettes, or a light, the pledge would have to dig through the stocking to find the requested object, and in the course of so doing, the egg often broke. "The egg, which each pledge was required to carry and which each pledge broke at least once, served as an ordeal when it broke. The raw egg, when broken either ran all over the contents of the stocking or dripped down the leg of the pledge, or both." (1972:150). At one lineup, the fraternity member in charge of the pledges ordered two of them "to wipe the raw eggs from their legs" (1972:166). Leemon fails to comment on the possible significance of this hazing ritual, but it is surely relevant that nylon stockings are worn by women, not men, just as it may be significant that eggs are produced by females (chickens), not males. The process of boys becoming men thus involves carrying "female" eggs without breaking them. Moreover, the color and consistency of egg white dripping down a pledge's leg would seem to suggest the telltale evidence of what could be construed as the results of uncontrolled onanistic activity.

An even more overt manifestation of ritual sodomizing is a "Dog Pile," in which people pile up on top of each other on one unfortunate victim who commits a foolish act (UC Berkeley, 1992). Dog piling is also reported elsewhere (Rhoads 1995:318), and it is known by other names, such as "the heap" (Sanday 1990:55). When a fraternity member is deemed to have acted imprudently, someone grabs him, throws him to the ground, preferably on his stomach, and cries out, "Bufu!" to signal others to jump on top of the victim to form the Dog Pile. While this description alone conveys homosexual rape, the etymology of "bufu," butt fuck, leaves no doubt about the symbolism. A revealing account of life in the Duke University chapter of Delta Tau Delta includes a brother suggesting that a pledge "Butt fuck a quad dog" (DeParle 1988:43).

This same act is also depicted verbally in the term "buddy-fucking" which means to engage in an act that is "unbrotherly" or disruptive to group harmony, such as making a point to show oneself as superior to others (endeavoring to succeed where others have failed) or by secretly dating another member's girlfriend. Thus, in this case, being humiliated is equated with passive homosexual intercourse. It is an insulting term because the humiliation does not occur in the context of hazing, in which it is acceptable to feminize the pledges. The same is true for the unflattering terms "mind-fuck," when one person mentally harasses another (Berkeley, 1987), or "rat fuck" (Berkeley, 1987; rat was the house members' nickname), which means to interrupt someone's life with a prank that falls outside of hazing.

Men's fears about masculinity often center on the penis. The question arises whether it will function adequately in a heterosexual act. This is why many of the hazing practices tend to pose apparent threats to the initiates' organs. In "the brick," a pledge goes to a roof, cliff, or other high place and must allow members of the fraternity to tie a rope to the end of his penis. The other end of the rope is tied to a brick (or in some versions, a rock). Although it turns out that the rope is either longer than the drop or the rope is cut before the brick hits the ground, the goal is to threaten the credulous pledge with losing his sex organ. Although this practice may be a legend (that is, fictitious but told as true), it nevertheless serves as an example of how fraternities use emasculation, threatened or real, as part of their initiation. The same ritual has been reported in 1986 as a component of a Coast Guard initiation. The neophytes were required to tie a line of string to their penises or testicles. Attached to the other end of the line was a five-to-eight-pound shackle. The initiates were then ordered to throw the "Shackle of Truth." Unbeknownst to them, the string had been cut. Each initiate grimaced in anticipation of acute pain as he threw down the shackle (Nuwer 1990:205). It should be noted that some rituals do involve actual physical discomfort, as in the case of a rookie Canadian hockey player who had a bucket tied to his penis with a hockey skate lace. The bucket was then hung over a hockey stick that was resting across the backs of two chairs. The apparent objective was for the veterans to slowly throw pucks into the bucket, pulling on the rookie's penis, until the rookie could make the veteran players laugh" (Bryshun 1997:68).

Quite a number of hazing practices center on the male organ. One such practice reported from Beta Theta Pi had the initiates rousted out of bed around ten o'clock at night. They were ordered to take off all their

Fraternity Initiation through Infantilization and Feminization   117

clothes and were then each given an onion tied to a piece of string. The string was placed around each initiate's neck with the loose end tied to his organ. The onion hung down on the other side. Any time a senior member of the fraternity wanted to speak to an initiate, he would pull the onion and that action would cause one's organ to rise (symbolizing an erection?). The initiates were not allowed to speak unless someone pulled their onion. The initiates were also told that if ordered to take a bite of the onion, they would have to do so. A version of this ritual reported from Valparaiso University in Indiana in the 1960s is referred to as "The Old 'Onion Yank' Trick" (Egan 1985:61). (Perhaps biting the onion would have brought tears to their eyes, and boys are not supposed to cry. Only girls cry! In this context, it is noteworthy that a study of high school sororities in the early 1960s reported that a pledge was ordered to cry as part of the hazing process. Members screamed at the pledge to help make her cry, but if she failed to do so, she was de-pledged [Schwartz and Merten 1968:1124].) The Beta Theta Pi initiates would be dismissed and put back in bed only to be awakened a half-hour later for the same procedure. They would have to again disrobe, find their onion, tie it to their penis, throw the onion over their neck, and line up again for a repeat of the ordeal. This could continue on through the night (Raphael 1988:83–84). Sometimes tears may be justified when actual pain is felt, as might occur in the case of the common practice of rubbing Ben-Gay on the pledges' testicles (Sanday 1990:167, Matthews 1997:88).

We have already commented on the fact that it was considered humiliating for a pledge to have an erection while in the presence of males, such a condition being construed by the group as a revealing telltale sign of nascent homosexual tendencies. A Berkeley student in 1983 reported a ritual known as the "Woody Check." The ritual consisted of active members of a fraternity arising in the middle of the night to enter the sleeping quarters of the pledges. They sneak into the rooms and rip off the covers of the bed of each pledge, checking to see whether or not they have erections or "woodies." It would certainly be highly embarrassing to be suddenly wakened to find that one had an erection that was being observed by a dozen or so of one's fraternity brothers. At Indiana University in 1931, Lockridge describes a scene where the pledges were ordered to sit on the floor naked with their legs spread. Then a senior member of the fraternity read aloud to the pledges selections from a pornographic text, for example, *Nights in a Harem,* while the other fraternity members "gathered around to monitor erections. Bets were placed and an incipient erection was cheered and hooted" (Lockridge 1994:98).

From this presentation of traditional fraternity hazing rituals, we can see that there are definite, consistent patterns of imagery and behavior. Previous studies of such rituals have sought to explain their function, for instance, producing male bonding, to help sever the conventional dependence of individuals on their natal families, providing a sense of belonging to a new, social, often prestigious group in what is sometimes perceived as an unfriendly or overwhelming atmosphere, and preparing young men for the ups and downs they are likely to encounter in life after leaving college. These studies all make valid points about the function of fraternity hazing. There also have been countless attempts to curtail hazing, usually unsuccessful. This includes a website, StopHazing.org. Certainly the brutal, sadistic punishment undergone by pledges, sometimes leading to lasting injuries and even death, are deplorable. But the patterns we have identified in this essay seem not to be have been much discussed by other students of hazing. The various techniques employed to infantilize the pledges, to reduce them to the level of naked un-toilet-trained infants who have to be force-fed and bathed as a means of facilitating their "rebirth" as full-fledged "older" brothers instead of remaining in a state of enforced babyhood, are critical, we feel, to a more comprehensive understanding of fraternity hazing. Many have correctly observed that fraternity initiations involve a form of "symbolic rebirth" (Kimmel 1996:173), but what has not been stressed enough, in our opinion, is that the rebirth ritual often entails forcing the initiates to assume the position of helpless infants unable to feed themselves or control their bowels.

Male fraternity initiations involve not only infantilization but feminization as well. Infantilization and feminization are both techniques designed to humiliate the initiates, and these techniques are not mutually exclusive. Women, after all, have long been infantilized by males who insist on calling them "baby," "babe," "babycakes," or "baby-doll." Even "chick" (baby chicken) is part of the pattern. While it is undeniably true that fraternity rituals tend to demean women as sex objects, the labeling of pledges as "girls," insisting that they perform menial "women's" tasks around the fraternity house, and coercing them to wear

Fraternity Initiation through Infantilization and Feminization

women's undergarments and cosmetics seem to be attempts to demean the pledges, not women. The demeaning of women is a by-product of this effort (and, to be sure, a sad reflection of the male chauvinist values held by too many American men). The various comments by earlier scholars to the effect that there are homoerotic elements in fraternity rituals are on target, but they are not the whole story. It is the fear of young boys that they may be or appear to be homosexuals that pervades many of the hazing rituals. It would perhaps be more accurate, then, to say that homophobic elements also are an element in fraternity traditions. The homophobic actions may well mask a basic homoerotic aspect of young men voluntarily living together in close quarters (Sanday 1990:122, Windmeyer and Freeman 1998). Many of the hazing rituals serve to make public what has hitherto been strictly private. Masturbation is normally a solitary activity, but in the fraternity context, it becomes a public act, often involving mutual masturbation, or masturbation in concert.

In the light of this analysis, it would seem that hazing with all of its self-conscious grossness and its infliction of mental and physical duress on an unending series of pledge cohorts functions to do much more than merely provide a means of male bonding. The content of the hazing rituals deals with the necessity of putting aside the conventional norms of childhood and accepting the ideals of gender identity as determined by a group of age-grade peers, painful though that process may be. The process includes being forced to act regressively as an unsocialized infant as well as being compelled to symbolically shed any remnant of "female" or "feminine" values or behavior. From the perspective of the imposers of hazing, the psychological benefits are obvious. The more the initiates are infantilized, the greater the distance between them and the senior members of the fraternity who are acting as pseudoparent surrogates, that is, "adults." Similarly, the more the initiates are feminized, the more macho or masculine the senior members appear to be by comparison.

An initiation ritual described by Sanday shows elements of both infantilization and feminization quite clearly. The pledges were first forced to wear diapers and were "hosed down with buckets of red sticky liquid" (doubtless representing menstrual blood). Then the pledges cleaned up the mess and removed their diapers to expose their genitals to the ridicule of the brothers. "Their diapers were then replaced and makeup and perfume were applied to the pledges" (1990:159). And this is how hazing is supposed to transform uninitiated boys into mature young men.

References Cited

Baier, John L., and Patrick S. Williams. 1983. Fraternity Hazing Revisited: Current Alumni and Active Member Attitudes Toward Hazing. *Journal of College Student Personnel* 24:300–305.
Bronner, Simon J. 1990. *Piled Higher and Deeper: The Folklore of Campus Life*. Little Rock: August House.
Bryshun, Jamie. 1997. *Hazing in Sport: An Exploratory Study of Veteran/Rookie Relations*. Master's thesis in Sociology. University of Calgary.
Buchanan, E. T., et al. 1982. Hazing: Collective Stupidity, Insensitivity and Irresponsibility. *NASPA Journal* 20(1):56–68.
Carus, Paul. 1909. Hazing and Fagging. *Open Court* 23:430–37.
Chodorow, Nancy. 1979. *The Reproduction of Mothering: Psychoanalysis and the Sociology of Gender*. Berkeley and Los Angeles: University of California Press.
Colton, Larry. 1993. *Goat Brothers*. New York: Doubleday.
DeParle, Jason. 1988. About Men: About Cold Beer, Willing Women, Hazing, Conformity—About Fraternities. *Washington Monthly* 20(10):38–48.
Egan, Robert. 1985. *From Here to Fraternity*. New York: Bantam Books.
Eisenhart, R. Wayne. 1975. You Can't Hack It Little Girl: A Discussion of the Covert Psychological Agenda of Modern Combat Training. *Journal of Social Issues* 31(4):13–23.
Ford, Richard. 1986. Rules of the House. *Esquire* 105(6):231–34.
Gist, Noel P. 1940. Secret Societies: A Cultural Study of Fraternalism in the United States. *University of Missouri Studies* 15(4):1–184.
Hall, B. H. 1968. *A Collection of College Words and Customs*. Detroit: Gale Research Company.
Hirsch, Kathleen. 1990. Fraternities of Fear: Gang Rape, Male Bonding, and the Silencing of Women. *Ms.* 1(2):52–56.
Hutchinson, Horace G. 1896. Fags and Fagging. *Cornhill Magazine* 1:237–45.
Kimmel, Michael. 1996. *Manhood in America: A Cultural History*. New York: Free Press.
Kopay, David, and Perry Deane Young. 1977. *The David Kopay Story*. New York: Arbor House.
La Fontaine, J. S. 1985. *Initiation: Ritual Drama and Secret Knowledge Across the World*. Harmondsworth: Penguin Books.
Larguèze, Brigitte. 1995. Statut des Filles et Représentations Féminines dans les Rituels de Bizutage. *Sociétés Contemporaines* 21:75–88.
Leemon, Thomas A. 1972. *The Rites of Passage in a Student Culture*. New York: Teachers College Press.
Legman, Gershon. 1968. *Rationale of the Dirty Joke: An Analysis of Sexual Humor*. New York: Grove Press.
———. 1975. *No Laughing Matter*. New York: Breaking Point.
Leslie, Joanne, Mark L. Taff, and Michael Mulvihill. 1985. Forensic Aspects of Fraternity Hazing. *American Journal of Forensic Medicine and Pathology* 6:53–67.
Lewis, Jan. 1991. Fraternity Hazing: Is That Any Way to Treat a Brother? *Trial* 27(9):63–66.
Lockridge, Larry. 1994. *Shade of the Raintree: The Life and Death of Ross Lockridge, Jr.* New York: Viking Penguin.
Matthews, Anne. 1996. Hazing Days. *New York Times Magazine*, Nov. 3, pp. 50–51.
———. 1997. *Bright College Years: Inside the American Campus Today*. New York: Simon & Schuster.
Merton, Andrew. 1985. Return to Brotherhood. *Ms.* 14(3):60, 62–64, 121–22.
Morris, Willie. 1967. *North Toward Home*. Boston: Houghton Mifflin.
Nuwer, Hank. 1990. *Broken Pledges: The Deadly Rite of Hazing*. Atlanta: Longstreet Press.
———. 1999. *Wrongs of Passage: Fraternities, Sororities, Hazing, and Binge Drinking*. Bloomington: Indiana University Press.

Fraternity Initiation through Infantilization and Feminization

———. 2000. *High School Hazing: When Rites Become Wrongs.* New York: Franklin Watts.
O'Hara, Jane. 2000. The Hell of Hazing. *Maclean's* 113 (10):50–52.
Olmert, Michael. 1983. Points of Origin. *Smithsonian* 14(6):150–54.
Ramzy, Ishak, and Keith Bryant. 1962. Notes on Initiation and Hazing Practices. *Psychiatry* 25:354–62.
Raphael, Ray. 1988. *The Men from the Boys: Rites of Passage in Male America.* Lincoln: University of Nebraska Press.
Rhoads, Robert A. 1995. Whales Tales, Dog Piles, and Beer Goggles: An Ethnographic Case Study of Fraternity Life. *Anthropology and Education Quarterly* 26:306–23.
Sanday, Peggy Reeves. 1990. *Fraternity Gang Rape.* New York: New York University Press.
Schwartz, Gary, and Don Merten. 1968. Social Identity and Expressive Symbols: The Meaning of an Initiation Ritual. *American Anthropologist* 70:1117–31.
Simmel, Georg. 1906. The Sociology of Secret Societies. *American Journal of Sociology* 11:441–98.
Steinberg, Neil. 1992. *If At All Possible, Involve a Cow: The Book of College Pranks.* New York: St. Martin's Press.
Sweet, Stephen. 1999. Understanding Fraternity Hazing: Insights from Symbolic Interactionist Theory. *Journal of College Student Development* 40:355–64.
Thwing, Charles F. 1878–79. College Hazing. *Scribner's Monthly* 17:331–33.
Tiger, Lionel. 1984. *Men in Groups.* 2nd ed. New York: Marion Boyars Publishers.
Van Gennep, Arnold. 1960. *The Rites of Passage.* Chicago: University of Chicago Press.
Vargas, Elizabeth (Anchor). 2000. Breaking Boys: Incidents of hazing becoming more violent and sexual. ABC News transcript: 20/20 Downtown, June 1, 2000. Reporter: Chris Cuomo.
Webster, Hutton. 1968. *Primitive Secret Societies.* 2nd ed. New York: Octagon Books.
Windmeyer, Shane L., and Pamela W. Freeman, eds. 1998. *Out on Fraternity Row: Personal Accounts of Being Gay in a College Fraternity.* Los Angeles: Alyson Books.
Wright, Esther. 1996. *Torn Togas: The Dark Side of Campus Greek Life.* Minneapolis: Fairview Press.
Young, Frank W. 1965. *Initiation Ceremonies: A Cross-Cultural Study of Status Dramatization.* Indianapolis: Bobbs-Merrill.

7

The Greek Game of *Makria Yaidoura* [Long Donkey]

AN ADOLESCENT ARTICULATION OF A MEDITERRANEAN MODEL OF MASCULINITY

In the December 29, 1883, issue of the *Athenaeum,* J. Theodore Bent reported "Some Games played by modern Greeks," a brief note that was reprinted the very next year in the *Folk-Lore Journal.* One of the games he observed on the island of Samos was called "How many?" He described it as follows:

> Four, six, or more lads divide themselves into sides, choosing two leaders. One leader takes up a stone, the other guesses in which hand it is, and if he is wrong, he and his party turn their backs to be mounted by their opponents. The leader, as soon as he has jumped on the back of the opponent leader, puts one hand over the eyes of his *zoon* (animal) or beast of burden, as he is termed, and with the other catches him a smart cuff on the head as a sign of subjection. After that he holds up as many fingers in the air as he likes, crying "How many?" and the *zoon* has to guess. One after the other they receive a cuff on the head, and have to guess, until at length a happy *zoon* is right, and the riders become the beasts of burden. (Bent 1884:58)

In a version reported from Chios in 1949, the leader of the boys on the backs of the others recites: *Araï bouraï,* / In the courtyard of the butcher, / They have planted a lemon tree. / Lemon tree, orange tree. / How many pieces of wood are there on the mountains?" (or as an alternative: "How many apples are there on the apple tree?"). While reciting this formula,

The Greek Game of *Makria Yaidoura* [Long Donkey]   123

he holds up his fingers to indicate the number of pieces of wood. If the boy he is riding, who cannot see, guesses the number correctly, his team goes on the backs of the other. Otherwise they continue until he guesses (Argenti and Rose 1949:2:1021).

In the year 2000, Kristina van Niekerk, an undergraduate student in my introductory folklore course collected an account of *Makria Yaidoura* (Long Donkey) from a twenty-nine-year-old male who had learned the game at age ten, circa 1981, from his neighborhood peers in Holargos, a suburb of Athens. Here is the essence of her detailed report:

The game is played with a minimum of about 8 players who divide themselves into two even teams, requiring a wall as a necessary component. Although not demanding a large amount of space, the game is played outdoors. The object of the game is to collapse the structure formed by the bodies of the opposing team, team A, by using the body mass of the members of team B.

The game is played as follows: One member of the first team, team A, stands in front of a wall, facing it. Keeping both legs straight, the player bends forward from the waist until his back is horizontal to the ground. Usually the player then fully extends both arms straight over the head and presses the palms of his hands flat against the wall. The rest of team A position themselves in a line behind the first player, standing behind one another in the same bent-over position as the first player. The players then wrap their arms around the waist of the team member immediately in front of them—placing their heads to either the left or right side of that member's buttocks—until all of team A create a long platform with their flattened backs extending perpendicularly away from the wall.

Team B then lines up a few yards behind team A, which extends in a straight line directly in front of them. One by one, each member of team B runs and jumps, vaulting over the buttocks of the last member of team A to land sitting astride the platform formed from team A's flattened backs. The first members of team B attempt to jump as far forward as possible so as to leave room for their fellow team members. Making room for all of team B's players is a strategy designed to take full advantage of the players' combined weight, a technique which is more likely to succeed in collapsing team A's structure thereby "winning" the round. After landing, the members of team B may not shift their position further up along the structure. The jumping team B players may grab onto the opposing team A player beneath them, but if any team B player touches the ground with hands or feet, or falls off the "long donkey," then the player is "out" for that particular round. Similarly, a team A player may not touch the ground with a hand to prevent himself from collapsing beneath the jumping player as this act would cause all of team A to lose that round.

Several different strategies are employed in the playing of the game. One of team B's ploys would involve trying to land on the weakest parts of a team A player such as the arms or shoulders rather than the hips. The hips of an A player would provide more support because the weight of the team B player would be centered more over the team A player's legs. Another technique would be to attempt to have several team B players land on a particularly vulnerable part of team A's structure, for example, on the smallest or weakest members of team A. This would offer a greater chance of collapsing the "long donkey" and thus defeating team A. Team A might seek to counter this last tactic by placing their weakest members nearer the wall where not only would the weakest have the extra support afforded by the wall, but it would also be much less likely that team B members could reach the backs of these weaker players on the initial jump onto the "long donkey."

According to the informant, the two teams would switch places when either team B collapses team A's "long donkey" which would give team B the point, or after all the members of team B have jumped and failed to collapse team A's structure which would give team A the point. The game would be played until time ran out, and then the points would be tallied to determine the final winner.

The same game is found in Turkey, often bearing the same name, "Long Donkey" (Brewster 1945, 1953:118), a name which was reported as early as 1694 (Opie and Opie 1969:261). Here is a Turkish version of *Uzun Essek* (The Long Donkey) reported in 1970 by my student Bora Özkök, who learned it at his home in Adana. Played only by boys ranging from ages eight to eighteen, two teams are formed with from three to seven players on each team. The two teams together elect a *Yastik* (pillow), a boy who will act as the referee as well as a "pillow." A coin may be flipped to decide which team is "going under" first. The team that loses the coin flip begins to line up behind the *Yastik*. They will form the donkey.

The Greek Game of *Makria Yaidoura* [Long Donkey] 125

The *Yastik* stands with his back against a wall or tree, and the losing team lines up behind him. The first boy puts his head halfway between the Yastik's legs under his crotch and grabs hold of the Yastik's knees. The second boy lines up behind the first, puts his head halfway between the first boy's legs underneath his crotch, and grabs hold of the first boy's knees. The rest of the team follows this same pattern until they are all lined up.

The other team lines up at some distance behind the "donkey," with the best jumper in front. That boy runs up and, as in "leap frog" or as a cowboy mounting his horse from the rear in western motion pictures, he uses his hands to spring off the last boy in the donkey's back and jumps over the backs of as many boys as he can (so as to leave as much room as possible for the other members of his team). As in the Greek version, the smallest and weakest boys are lined up at the front of the donkey for fear that they will not be able to hold up the weight of the jumping team. If they are not strong enough, the donkey will collapse and the same team will have to go under again. Sometimes, a smaller boy will ask to be placed at the back of the donkey to show to his comrades that he can bear the weight and not let his team down. By doing this, he gains respect from the group.

In succession, each of the other boys runs and jumps onto the "donkey" until they are all sitting on its back. The referee, during every jump, watches carefully to see whether the jumper's feet touch the ground. Even if one boy's feet barely touch, if the *Yastik* sees it, the whole jumping team is disqualified and must go underneath.

When everyone is mounted, the team on top chants this rhyme (cf. Brewster 1965:363):

Bizim	köyün	inamï	
The preacher	of our	village	
Alttan	verir	samanï	
Give	the straws (hay)	underneath	
Üstten	cikar	dumanï	
Smoke	comes from	the top	
Attï	attï	kac	attï?
Flip,	flip,	what do we	flip?

At the conclusion of the chanting, the captain of the mounted team signals with the fingers of his hand a number from one to five. The last line

126   The Greek Game of *Makria Yaidoura* [Long Donkey]

of the chanted rhyme asks the question "What is the number?" Now the bottom captain must guess what the number is. If the guess is not correct, all the top team members scream out "Nooooooo" and shout for joy because they can remain on top for another round. If the guess had been correct, the mounted team would have had to go underneath to be the "donkey."

One strategy employed consists of the jumping team piling up on one boy. This is accomplished by having the first jumping boy lying flat after he completes his jump. The next boy springs high into the air and jumps on top of his teammate and also lies flat to provide a platform for the next jumper. The objective is to make the donkey collapse. This is called *Essek Çöktü* (donkey collapse). They do this because they do not want to give the donkey team a chance to guess the number of fingers held up. One danger in this piling-up technique is that each boy has to be able to jump high enough in the air so as to land in the middle of his teammate's back to add to the weight on one of the donkey boys. In a pile-up, the higher the pile gets, the more delicate the balance becomes. If any member of the jumping team's feet touch the ground, the round is lost. In a similar Turkish version of the game from Izmir, the rules state that the maximum number of points a team can earn in a round is one. The game continues until one team reaches an arbitrarily agreed upon number, for example, five or ten points.

There are literally dozens of versions of this game in print, and the details of play are remarkably consistent. My colleague Stanley Brandes reports a version he collected during his fieldwork in Andalusia. This Spanish version is known as *jugar a churro* (playing *churro*, a *churro* being a long skinny pastry). In this version, the "pillow" is termed *madre* (mother). The donkey in this case is a *mula,* or female mule. (It is noteworthy that whereas the Greek word for "donkey" is usually used in a neutral fashion, the term in the Greek game cited above adopts the female form *Yaidoura*.)

Here is Brandes's account:

> To form the *mula,* the *madre* stands against a lamppost or wall, facing outward. A member of the opposing team bends forward, burying his head in the *madre*'s stomach. The other members of his team attach themselves to one another in a long line, each boy bent forward and wrapping his arms

The Greek Game of *Makria Yaidoura* [Long Donkey]   127

around the waist of the boy in front. The boys' backs form a platform; the whole formation is known as the *mula*.

Members of the *madre*'s team now proceed to "mount" the *mula*, doing so by running from behind a base line and jumping on top of "her." All sorts of rules at this point come into play to determine which team wins. The members of the *madre*'s team (unlike the *mula*, this team has no special denomination) must all try to get on top of the *mula*. Thus, those who mount first try to position themselves as far forward as possible, a difficult task because players must remain at the spot where they land when they leap onto the *mula*. According to the rules, team members can mount atop one another too, thereby creating tiers of players, all sustained by the *mula*. As each mounter runs, he must call out, !*Churro*! He can also shout this term just prior to leaping. Forgetting to say the word at all means that his team automatically loses. The team also loses if a player's feet touch the ground while leaping and mounting. At the same time, should the *mula* cave in—that is, should the team on bottom lose grip of one another and collapse to the ground—the *mula* loses. For this reason, it is often the strongest or heaviest mounter who goes last. This player is supposed to land hard on the *mula* just at the point that it is carrying the greatest weight, thus causing it to collapse.

If the *mula* fails to cave in, a self-appointed representative of the *madre*'s team raises a certain number of fingers in a predetermined signal. Any one of the players constituting the *mula*, his head of course bent toward the ground, instantly guesses which signal that might be, that is, how many fingers his opponent is holding up. The *madre*, who faces both teams, acts as impartial observer and declares whether the player has guessed correctly. If he has guessed correctly, the two teams change roles, the players who mounted now becoming the *mula*. If not, the teams assume the same roles as before. To be among the *mula* is a physically trying, undesirable role. The object of the game is to mount, never to be mounted. The *madre*, unless "she" quits, continues to play as long as the game stays in effect or someone else assumes the position. (1993:126–27)

In different versions of the game, the animal mounted varies. In the United States, one version of this traditional game is called "Johnny on the Pony" (Brewster 1945, 1953:116–18). One English version found in the second volume of Lady Gomme's standard collection of games, first published in 1898, was titled "Saddle the Nag" (Gomme 1964:2:147). The Opies cite a host of traditional names of the game, including "Leap the

128 The Greek Game of *Makria Yaidoura* [Long Donkey]

Horse," "Camel's Back," "All Aboard," "All on the Horses," "Jump the Long Horse," "Jump the Long Mare," "Long-Tailed Nag," "Weak Horses," "Strong Horses, Weak Donkeys," "Iron Donkeys," and "Donkey Jump" (Opie and Opie 1969:257–60). Keeping in mind that "cuddy" is an old traditional nickname for donkey, we can appreciate such additional names of the game as "Bump a Cuddy," "Cuddie's Weight," "Cuddie gi[v]e Way," "Jump the Cuddie," "Munt-a-cuddy," and "Funking Cuddie" (258). In India, the game is known as "Tell me how many eggs?" (Brewster 1943a), but in one version the winner taunts the loser by saying "Horse mine; pony yours." This refers to the fact that higher status individuals ride horses whereas poor people ride ponies. In another version from India, the line formed by those being ridden is termed a "Ghodi" or mare (Brewster 1955:93–94).

As Brandes correctly observes (1993:127n1), the game he described is definitely a version of "How Many Horns Has the Buck?" It is of considerable antiquity and has been the subject of several scholarly essays (Collin 1918, Ullman 1943). Notable especially is Paul Brewster's elaborate assemblage of versions initially published in *Béaloideas: Journal of the Folklore of Ireland Society* in 1942, a Dutch translation of which appeared in *Volkskunde* (Brewster 1944–45). The original *Béaloideas* essay was reprinted in 1965.

One of the earliest allusions to the game occurs in the famous *Satyricon* of Petronius Arbiter, who died in 66 A.D. An incident in the memorable "Cena Trimalchionis" tells how a scuffle between a boy and a dog results in the dinner table candle being overturned, causing the breakage of crystal glasses. The host, Trimalchio, seems unconcerned at this. He kisses the boy and orders him to get on his back. Once astride his master's back, the boy slaps Trimalchio's shoulders and cries, "Bucca bucca, quot sunt hic?" The words are assumed by most scholars to be cognate with those found in English versions of the game "Buck, buck, how many (fingers, horns) do I hold up?" or the German "Bock, Bock, wieviel Hörner hab ich?" (Opie and Opie 1969:299). None other than E. B. Tylor, one of the founding fathers of the discipline of anthropology, noted the parallel between the English versions and the text cited by Petronius. In the first volume of his *Primitive Culture*, first published in 1871, Tylor remarks: "We may see small schoolboys in the lanes playing at the guessing-game, where one gets on another's back and holds up fingers, the other must guess how many. It is interesting to note the wide distribution and long permanence of these trifles in history when we read the passage from Petronius Arbiter, written in the time of Nero" (1958:74). One might question Tylor's unnecessarily demeaning labeling of the game as a "trifle" in history, for as we hope to demonstrate, the game provides an important metaphorical articulation of ideal masculinity in Mediterranean and for that matter Indo-European cultures.

Certainly, the antiquity and continuity of the game over the centuries is not in dispute. There are even visual records of the game. In Peter Bruegel's famous 1560 *Children's Games,* housed in the Kunsthistorisches Museum in Vienna, we find in the lower right-hand corner a version in which two boys are riding two other boys, with first boy of the "donkey" placing his head in the lap of a "pillow" boy, facing outward, sitting on the edge of a wooden bench or table. The second of the two riders is holding up the fingers of his left hand. (For a photograph of the game in England, see the plate facing page 256 in the Opies' *Children's Games in Street and Playground.*)

Extrapolating from Brewster's compilation of more than eighty versions of the game, we may distinguish two basic subtypes of the game (cf. Brewster 1943b:135). The first subtype, the simpler one, involves just two boys. One is the rider and one is the ridden. The presence of a "pillow" is optional. Some versions of this subtype have a third boy serving as pillow; some do not. The second subtype involves teams as described above in the Greek, Turkish, and Spanish versions. Once again, a pillow or referee may be found in this subtype.

Both subtypes or forms of the game are mentioned in Basile's celebrated collection of Neapolitan folktales, first published from 1634 to 1636. At the beginning of the second day's tales contained in the *Pentamerone,* Basile includes an extended list of thirty-one traditional games, evidently played in Naples. One is called *Anca Nicola* and is described as follows: "It consists of one boy bending over and putting his head in the lap of another, who then with his hands hides the eyes of the first. A third boy then jumps astride on his back and sings: *Anca Nicola, si' bella e si' bona, E si' maretata: Quanta corna tiene ncapa?* Putting a hand on his hand and raising as many fingers as he wishes. The boy under him has to guess without seeing the number of fingers" (Penzer 1932:1:131n3). If the boy guesses the number of *corne* (horns) incorrectly; the game continues until he guesses correctly. Basile also lists *Travo luongo*, or "Long Beam," that Penzer compares to *a cavallo luongo* (long horse) (1:133n21). This second game corresponds to the team versions of "How Many Horns Has the Buck?"

One question about the game that has hitherto not been answered concerns the significance, if any, of the presence of the word "horns" in the most common verbal formula accompanying the game action. Of course, "horns" refers to the fingers held up by the rider, the number of which is to be guessed by the person or persons being ridden. But the possible symbolic significance of "horns" in the game has thus far eluded folkloristic inquiry.

In adult life in Mediterranean cultures, horns have a definite connotation, a rather negative one. There are various folk metaphorical expressions and customs that show without a doubt that for a man to give another man horns is to indicate that the horned one has been cuckolded. In Portugal, for example, "the placing of horns upon the door or house of a married man is considered a most atrocious insult" (Hornell 1925:309). The same source indicates that "a door daubed with a rude drawing of a man's head carrying horns . . . is the subject of innumerable vulgar jokes" (309). It is a pity that Hornell did not bother to record and report these "vulgar jokes," but fortunately, a courageous American female anthropologist did include a number of cuckold jokes in her remarkable collection of modern Greek folklore (Orso 1979:93–95), correctly annotating several of them under the rubric of Motif H 425.2, Horns grow on cuckold. She also remarks that the cuckold is "a common theme in Greek culture" (65–66). The term in Italian for a deceived husband is *cornuto*, while in French it is *cornute*. In modern Greek, the term *keratás* means literally "horned one" but metaphorically means cuckold (Koukoules 1983:157). Accordingly, "he puts horns on him" means "he made a cuckold out of him" (177).

A remarkable bit of anecdotal evidence confirms the symbolic significance of "horns" in a modern Greek context. On January 28, 1867, an incident took place on Kerkyra, one of the Ionian islands. Peasant sharecroppers cultivating the land of absentee landlords were scheduled on that day to pay their rents. Failure to do so risked detention in prison until the debt was paid. As the peasants approached the bailiffs who were surrounded by constables, sitting behind tables in a village square, most

The Greek Game of *Makria Yaidoura* [Long Donkey]   131

carried baskets filled with olives while others were unable to pay the rent. Suddenly, an unidentified man appeared with a basket on his shoulder and came forward, presumably to make his rent payment. When his basket's contents were revealed, the assembled crowd roared with laughter. The basket did not contain olives or grapes or currants but rams' horns. As Gallant, who described this event, remarked, "No further rents were collected that day, as the humiliated bailiffs and their erstwhile guardians fled" (Gallant 1994:703). Gallant went on to explain the reason for the humiliation. "The throwing down of the horns symbolized the cuckolding of the landlords, or in this case, their representatives. In a reversal of roles, the rent/wife was now in the hands of the lover/tenants; and there she would remain. And so the husband/landlords had been proclaimed impotent and were worthy only of the derisive laughter which mocked their public shame" (704).

Further confirmation of the horns-cuckold equation, if any were needed, is provided by the widespread distribution of the vertical and horizontal "horn sign." A study based on 1,200 informants from forty locations indicated that 515 of them understood the vertical horn-sign as signifying cuckold while only 29 interpreted it as a general insult and 10 as an apotropaic form of protection (Morris et al. 1979:120). The horizontal horn-sign meanings included 368 for cuckold with 86 for protection (136). Even the protective aspect of both signs can be construed to have phallic implications. Typically, the gesture is used to ward off the adverse effects of the evil eye (Dundes 1980:93–133). Inasmuch as the evil eye can have a desiccating impact, for example, drying up body fluids, the horns are presumably employed to counteract this threat of impotence. In Italy, a male fearful of being struck by the evil eye may touch his testicles as a prophylactic technique. (Spitting is an alternative means of demonstrating male virility, that is, the ability to produce liquid.)

Now the reader may well wonder how the "horns" as a sign of cuckoldry could have anything to do with the game of "How Many Horns Has the Buck?" After all, the boys who play this game are not married and are therefore in no position to cuckold one another. The point is not that the horns signify cuckoldry in this instance, but rather that they are phallic symbols. An examination of the fourteen diverse theories proposed to explain how the equation "horns = cuckold" might have arisen (Morris et al. 1979:120–27) reveals that whether the horns are understood as those of a bull, or a stag, the basic message is that the addressee of the gesture lacks them. In other words, he is a male without horns, without a functioning phallus. It is the male making the gesture who has the horns and who is providing the horns for the addressee, for example, suggesting he or some other male is enjoying the wife of the addressee. In the context of our game, it is the rider or riders who possess the horns while those being ridden do not. The riders are masculine; those ridden are feminized. Men or boys without horns are analogous to women or girls.

To fully appreciate this distinction in a Greek environment, it is critical to understand the difference between attitudes toward active and passive homosexuals. In a homoerotic situation, the active homosexual is considered to be acting as a male while the passive homosexual is considered to be effeminate, acting like a female. This important distinction is not new but in fact is well attested in classical Greek culture (Slater 1968:61). In Athenian comedy, for example, males who walked slowly, wearing long tunics, were mocked as "being effeminates or passive homosexuals" (Bremmer 1992:19, Dover 1980:16, 68, 76, 135). The idea that there is no disgrace in being an active homosexual but a definite disgrace or dishonor in being a passive homosexual is found not only in modern Greece but throughout the Mediterranean area and beyond. In Arabic, for example, *Al-fa'il*—the "doer"—is not an object of contempt like *Al-Maful*—the "done" (Vanggaard 1972:122). This is essentially the same as the modern Greek idiom that insists that a man should always *pidhai*, "jump," rather than *pidhiete*, "be jumped," or, in other words, "Men should always penetrate, should never allow themselves to be penetrated" (Faubion 1993:220). (The choice of the Greek verb for "jump" would seem to be directly relevant to our game.) Similarly, "it was disgraceful for a man in ancient Scandinavia to be another man's underdog and to be used sexually as a woman by him" (Vanggaard 1972:77). As Brandes points out, part of the explanation of why men fear being cuckolded is that "to be cuckolded is to be transformed symbolically into a woman" (1980:90). Delaney clarifies the matter in a Turkish context: "the passive homosexual is the most shameful, not so much because of homosexuality, but because he has allowed himself to be put in the position of a woman" (1987:47n7). Certainly in modern Greek colloquial usage, the locution for an effeminate passive homosexual, *poustis*, is a strong insult (Herzfeld 1985:77, 158, Faubion 1993:223), though it can be a term of endearment between homosexual lovers (Koukoules 1983:170). It is worth noting that the longstanding critical difference in attitudes toward "active" and "passive" homosexuals is empirically verifiable regardless of whether or not ritual pederasty was ever actually practiced in ancient Greece as a form of male initiation (Bremmer 1980, Sergent 1987).

In classical Greece and elsewhere, the act of riding is deemed a metaphor for sexual intercourse (Dover 1980:59, Adams 1982:229), a metaphor current in modern Greek folklore. *Kavaldo* means literally "I ride" or "I mount" but is understood in slang usage to refer to intercourse (Koukoules 1983:154). What this suggests in terms of our game is that the boys on top are demonstrating their masculinity while those on the bottom are forced to occupy a passive, female position. The fingers (horns) held upright by the boys on top are phallic signals of masculinity. The fact that the boys on the bottom cannot see the "horns" is strangely reminiscent of the custom in which the vertical horn gesture signifying cuckold is commonly performed, often in jest, behind the victim's head (Driessen 1992:247) so that he cannot see it. Such a victim may feel compelled to try to guess why all his peers are suddenly laughing at him.

There is one more puzzling feature of the game that has perplexed those who have studied it: the word "bucca." In the first-century text founds in the *Satyricon*, the verbal formula is "Bucca, bucca, quot sunt hic?" The question is, what exactly does "Bucca, Bucca" mean? Collin in his 1918 essay says its meaning is uncertain, and he suggests that it might be the feminine form of a late Latin term *Bucco*, meaning *Dummkopf* or blockhead (1918:378–79). Ullman admits that the word in Latin means "cheek," but since the boy riding Trimalchio strikes him on the shoulders and not the cheek, *bucca*, he says, would appear to be "a nonsense word" (1943:96). Ullman argues that since there is a word for he-goat in many European languages that bears some similarity to the phonetic sound of "bucca," for example, *becco* in Italian, *bouc* in French, *Bock* in German, the Latin word *bucca* must also mean "goat." He even hopes, on the basis of his hypothetical reconstruction, that *bucca* in the sense of "he-goat" in Petronius will find its way into new editions of Latin dictionaries (1943:102).

Could the Latin meaning of "cheek" in the game make any sense at all? If the word "cheek" could refer to buttock as it does in English slang going back to the seventeenth century, then it would make perfect sense. The verbal formula would then read: "Cheek, cheek, how many are there?" The not so subtle allusion would be to anal penetration, an interpretation lent credence by Trimalchio's overt homosexual proclivity. We know from evidence from vase painting that even heterosexual intercourse in ancient Greece was often anal (Dover 1980:189). And we know also that in modern Mediterranean cultures, the threat of anal penetration is a standard part of male verbal dueling and joking (Brandes 1980:95). A study of Turkish adolescent male verbal dueling, for example, revealed the following general principle: "One of the most important goals is to force one's opponent into a female passive role. This may be done by defining the opponent or his mother or sister as a wanton sexual receptacle. If the male opponent is thus defined, it is usually by means of casting him as a submissive anus, an anus which must accept the brunt of the verbal duelist's attacking phallus (Dundes, Leach, and Özkök 1970:326). The duels are usually oral, but they may also occur as written graffiti: "This was written by Tosun; anybody who reads it is fucked by him" (341). We find a close parallel in a Modern Greek graffito: "The writer's prick / up the reader's ass" (Koukoules 1983:111). Even the most innocuous question can provide an opportunity to "stick it," so to speak, to one's opponent (Dundes, Leach, and Özkök 1970:330, Koukoules 1983:125). This tradition goes back at least two thousand years. Pompeian graffiti include such expressions as "pedicatur qui leget" meaning "He who reads this is suffering *pedicatio*" (Adams 1982:124–25).

Are we justified in interpreting the game of "How Many Horns Has the Buck?" as a parallel to Turkish and Greek verbal dueling? Consider several of the names of the game in England. One is "Husky-Bum, Finger or Thumb?" Others include "Rum-stick-a-bum, here I come," "Bung the Barrel," "Bum Bum Barrel," "Bumsy Barrels," and "Bung the Bucket" (Opie and Opie 1969:257–60). "Bum" is English slang for posterior, and "bunghole" is slang for asshole. These terms surely suggest an anal assault. Remember too that in the Greek text the donkey is a female donkey just as in the Andalusian version the mule is likewise a female. If we put all the data together, we can reasonably speculate that 'How Many Horns Has the Buck?" is a macho boast to a feminized rival, inviting "her" to guess just how many phalluses are threatening "her" anus. And even if we granted, for the sake of argument, Ullman's labored effort to insist that *Bucca* meant "goat" rather than "cheek," the fact is that "the deceived husband in Italy, Spain and Portugal is identified with the billy-goat (*becco, cabrón, cabrão*). The Italian term *becco* is a synonym of *cornuto*—husband of an unfaithful woman. In Spanish, too, *cornudo* and *cabrón* denote a man who consents to his wife's adultery" (Blok 1981:428). In a study of a Castilian rural community, Kenny observes (1962:83): "To call a man a 'buck' or 'he-goat' (*cabrón*) is the worst possible insult.... When referring to a cuckolded husband, it is said that he has been given 'horns.'" Adding this final piece of the puzzle, we may be able to say that the latent adult translation of the verbal formula "How Many Horns Has the Buck?" is "How many times has the 'goat' been cuckolded?"

We hope that it is now possible to see that Tylor was in error when he called the game of "How Many Horns Has the Buck?" a mere "trifle," for it is our contention that the game is a powerful adolescent articulation of the model of masculinity found in those cultures where the game is played. The male jousting is designed to socialize young boys into the behavioral norms expected of them. Specifically, if a boy wants to be manly, he must avoid being a passive victim of other males. Instead, he must display signs of his superior masculinity, even if it involves feminizing his male peers. As Brandes phrased it in his astute analysis of his Andalusian game: "The mounted mule symbolizes ... the denigrated female figuration, the dominated female below, and the feminized male subject to attack from behind" (1993:128). We are extending his analysis to Greek and other versions of the game. In addition, we might also remark on the implications of the game with respect to male constructions of female identity. Women, in such constructions, are clearly defined as sexual objects to be mounted by men. This may be why the game is rarely played by girls. Rather it is a game expressly designed to force boys to distinguish clearly between "active" and "passive," between "rider" and ridden," between "male" and "female".

References Cited

Adams, J. N. 1982. *The Latin Sexual Vocabulary*. London: Duckworth.

Argenti, Philip P., and H. J. Rose. 1949. *The Folk-Lore of Chios*. 2 vols. Cambridge: Cambridge University Press.

Bent, J. Theodore. 1884. Some Games Played by Modern Greeks. *Folk-Lore Journal* 2:57–59.

Blok, Anton. 1981. Rams and Billy-Goats: A Key to the Mediterranean Code of Honour. *Man* 16:427–40.

Brandes, Stanley. 1980. *Metaphors of Masculinity: Sex and Status in Andalusian Folklore.* Philadelphia: University of Pennsylvania Press.

———. 1993. Spatial Symbolism in Southern Spain. *Psychoanalytic Study of Society* 18:119–35.

Bremmer, Jan. 1980. An Enigmatic Indo-European Rite: Paederasty. *Arethusa* 13:279–98.

———. 1992. Walking, Standing, and Sitting in Ancient Greek Culture. In Jan Bremmer and Herman Roodenburg, eds., *A Cultural History of Gesture,* 15–35. Ithaca: Cornell University Press.

Brewster, Paul. 1943a. The "Kitte Ande Bol" Game of India. *Southern Folklore Quarterly* 7:149–52.

———. 1943b. A Roman Game and Its Survival on Four Continents. *Classical Philology* 38:134–37.

———. 1944–45. Hoeveel Hoornen heeft de Bok? Prolegomena tot een vergelijkende Studie over een kinderspel. *Volkskunde* 46:361–93.

———. 1945. Johnny on the Pony: A New York State Game. *New York Folklore Quarterly* 1:239–40.

———. 1953. *American Nonsinging Games.* Norman: University of Oklahoma Press.

———. 1955. A Collection of Games from India, with some Notes on Similar Games in Other Parts of the World. *Zeitschrift für Ethnologie* 80:88–102.

———. 1965. Some Notes on the Guessing Game, How Many Horns Has the Buck? In Alan Dundes, ed., *The Study of Folklore,* 338–68. Englewood Cliffs, N.J.: Prentice-Hall.

Collin, Carl S. R. 1918. Bucca, bucca, quot sunt hic? Beiträge zur Geschichte eines Kinderspieles. In *Studier tillegnade Esaias Tegnér,* 369–79. Lund: C. W. K. Gleerups Förlag.

Delaney, Carol. 1987. Seeds of Honor, Fields of Shame. In David D. Gilmore, ed., *Honor and Shame and the Unity of the Mediterranean.* 35–48. Washington, D.C.: American Anthropological Association.

Dover, K. J. 1980. *Greek Homosexuality.* New York: Vintage Books.

Driessen, Henk. 1992. Gestured Masculinity: Body and Sociability in Rural Andalusia. In Jan Bremmer and Herman Roodenburg, eds., *A Cultural History of Gesture,* 237–52. Ithaca: Cornell University Press.

Dundes, Alan. 1980. *Interpreting Folklore.* Bloomington: Indiana University Press.

Dundes, Alan, Jerry W. Leach, and Bora Özkök. 1970. The Strategy of Turkish Boys' Verbal Dueling Rhymes. *Journal of American Folklore* 83:325–49.

Faubion, James D. 1993. *Modern Greek Lessons.* Princeton: Princeton University Press.

Gallant, Thomas W. 1994. Turning the Horns: Cultural Metaphors, Material Conditions, and the Peasant Language of Resistance in Ionian Islands (Greece) during the Nineteenth Century. *Comparative Studies in Society and History* 36:702–19.

Gomme, Alice Bertha. 1964. *The Traditional Games of England, Scotland, and Ireland.* 2 vols. New York: Dover.

Herzfeld, Michael. 1985. *The Poetics of Manhood: Contest and Identity in a Cretan Mountain Village.* Princeton: Princeton University Press.

Hornell, James. 1925. Horns in Madeiran Superstition. *Journal of the Royal Anthropological Institute of Great Britain and Ireland* 25:303–10.

Kenny, Michael. 1962. *A Spanish Tapestry: Town and Country in Castile.* Bloomington: Indiana University Press.

Koukoules, Mary. 1983. *Loose-Tongued Greeks: A Miscellany of Neo-Hellenic Erotic Folklore.* Paris: Digamma.

Morris, Desmond, et al. 1979. *Gestures: Their Origins and Distribution.* New York: Stein and Day.

Opie, Iona, and Peter Opie. 1969. *Children's Games in Street and Playground.* Oxford: Clarendon Press.

Orso, Ethelyn G. 1979. *Modern Greek Humor.* Bloomington: Indiana University Press.

Penzer, N. M., ed. 1932. *The Pentamerone of Giambattista Basile.* 2 vols. London: John Lane.

Sergent, Bernard. 1987. *Homosexuality in Greek Myth.* London: Athlone.

Slater, Philip. 1968. *The Glory of Hera: Greek Mythology and the Greek Family.* Boston: Beacon Press.

Tylor, Edward Burnett. 1958. *The Origins of Culture,* Part 1 of *Primitive Culture.* New York: Harper Torchbooks.

Ullman, B. L. 1943. Bucca, Bucca. *Classical Philology* 38:94–102.

Vanggaard, Thorkil. 1972. *Phallos: A Symbol and Its History in the Male World.* New York: International Universities Press.

EPILOGUE

Several years ago, the editors of *Who's Who in America* invited those individuals profiled in that volume to submit a personal closing statement under the rubric of "Thoughts on My Life." The statement was supposed to be a succinct autobiographical summary of the "principles, goals, ideals, and values that have been guidelines for success and achievement." Most individuals declined this unusual invitation, but a few took up the challenge, and their statements appear in italics following their formal list of degrees, honors, and publications.

I thought long and hard about what I might say, but secure in the knowledge that few if any of my colleagues or students would ever see how I evaluated my career, and with the added comfort of believing that anyone who really knew me would not really be surprised anyway, I composed the following: "As a psychoanalytic folklorist, my professional goals are to make sense of nonsense, find a rationale for the irrational, and seek to make the unconscious conscious." I bother to put this academic credo here because it is my sincere hope that the essays contained in this volume effectively represent some of my best efforts to reach the goals I set for myself.

INDEX

Aarne, Antti, 38
Abraham, Karl, 24
active vs. passive homosexual, 132, 135
Afanes'ev, A. N., 19
Aladdin, 71–72
Andersen, Hans Christian, 55–56, 58–59, 68
Arbesmann, Rudolph, 7
Aristotle, 86

Barber, Paul, 19
Basile, Giambattista, 129–30
Beit-Hallahmi, Benjamin, 3, 5
Bettelheim, Bruno, 50
blindness, as symbolic castration, 47
Bloody Mary, 76–94
Blumensohn, Jules, 8
Boas, Franz, 9
Brandes, Stanley, 126, 128, 132, 135
Bredsdorff, Elias, 55
Brewster, Paul, 128
Bronner, Simon J., 77–78, 87
Bufu, 115
buried alive, dread of being, 26

"Candy Ass trial," 105
castration, 10, 36, 47, 48–49, 62, 66, 67, 68, 69
catch, 100
Cinderella, 44
"Circle Jerk," 99
Cloud, Henry Roe, 8–9
cultural relativism, 5–6

de Vries, Jan, 37
death, as "debirth," 26, 28
defloration, 70–71
Delaney, Carol, 132
deus otiosus, 12–13
Devereux, George, 87
Dinnerstein, Dorothy, 62
"Dirty Swirl," 105
"Dog Lick," 98
"Dog Pile," 115
Dracula, 17, 26

Electra Complex, 61, 64, 72, 73
"Elephant Walk," 97–98, 107
Eliade, Mircea, 12
emasculation, threat of, 116. *See also* castration

fagging, 95
Farrell, Eileen, 9
fasting, 6–10
father projection, 4
Favazza, Armando R., 7–8, 10, 11
feminist critique, 59–60, 110
feminization, 96, 107–10, 111–13, 118–20
fetal position, 26
Fliess, Wilhelm, 41
folktale origins, Indianist theory of, 37
fork, symbolism of, 63, 68
Frazer, James George, 9
Freud, Sigmund, 3, 4, 5, 22–23, 26, 41–42, 43, 61, 64
Future of an Illusion, 3–4, 5–6

Gandhi, 7
gang bang, 110
gang shag, 110
Geertz, Clifford, 41
genital mutilation, female, 68–69
God, as father figure, 4–5
Goss, Michael, 88
Grimm, Jacob, 17–18
group rape, 110

hair, symbolism of, 100
Hansel and Gretel, 60
hazing, 95–121
high culture, 16
high gods, 12
Holbek, Bengt, 55
Hollis, Susan, 33, 34, 36, 37, 48, 50–51, 52
homosexuality, 58, 96, 97, 110, 113, 116, 117, 119, 132–33
Horálek, Karel, 33, 38, 39
Horney, Karen, 87
horns, symbolism of, 130–32

infantilization, 63, 102–07, 109, 111, 118, 119
Interpretation of Dreams, 26, 41–42
inverse projection. *See* projective inversion

Jack and the Beanstalk, 64
Jones, Ernest, 20, 23–24, 25, 26
Jung, Carl G., 61

Kardiner, Abram, 5–6, 13
King, Stephen, 91
Klein, Melanie, 24, 27
Kleinpaul, Rudolf, 23
Knapp, Mary and Herbert, 76–77
Kovel, Joel, 3
Krauss, Friedrich, 26
Krohn, Kaarle, 51
Kunstmärchen, 5

Lang, Andrew, 37
Langlois, Janet, 78–80, 86, 87
legend, definition of, 20, 57
lex talionis, 23, 25
limited good, principle of, 27
Linton, Ralph, 5
literal-historical approach, 19–20
"Little," as prefix, significance of, 63
Little Red Riding Hood, 60, 63
Long Donkey (game), 122–36

MacCulloch, J. A., 7
Maiden without Hands, 46
Mary Whales, 78–79, 86
Mary Worth, 77, 79, 85, 86, 87
masturbation, 71, 97, 99, 100, 119
"Mattress Toast," 104
Menninger, Karl, 7, 8, 10
menstruation, 84, 87, 90, 92
mermaid, 55–75
milk and honey, 27
Morphology of the Folktale, 58
Motif-Index of Folk-Literature, 18, 56
"Mulan," 72
Müller, Max, 4
myth, definition of, 38, 57
Myth of the Birth of the Hero, 43
myth-ritual interpretation, 51, 78

Nuwer, Hank, 101
Nwanunobi, Onyeka, 12

object loss, 25
object relation, 27, 28
Oedipus, 41–42, 61
Oedipus Complex, 48, 49, 52, 61, 64
oicotype, 38
"Olive Run," 114
omnipotence, of thought, 6, 9, 62
Onians, Richard Broxton, 21
"Onion Yank Trick," 117
oral sadism, 24, 25, 27, 28

paddling, as initiation practice, 102–03
penis envy, 66
Penzer, N. M., 40
performance theory, 76
Petronius Arbiter, 128, 129, 133–34
Pfister, Oskar, 3
"Pledge Sneak," 107
Pliny, 86
"Pocahontas," 72
Politis, N. G., 21
popular culture, 16–17
Potiphar's Wife motif, 36, 40, 42, 44, 46, 48, 50, 51
pranks, 95
projection, 23, 24, 26, 40–41, 43, 49, 50
projective inversion, 25, 40, 43–44, 46, 47, 49, 50
Propp, Vladimir, 44, 58
Psychopathology of Everyday Life, 41
"Pulling Train," 110
pussy, as insult, 109, 112

Rank, Otto, 43, 47, 49, 50
Raphael, Ray, 101
rite of passage, 92, 101
Robertson-Smith, W., 9
Rooth, Anna Birgitta, 38, 39

Sachs, Hanns, 49
Sanday, Peggy Reeves, 102, 110
Seduction Theory, 45
self-emasculation, 36, 38, 39, 46, 49
self-mutilation, 10–12

separation anxiety, 25
siren, 56, 57, 65
sissy, 110–11, 113
Slater, Philip, 13, 50
"Snow White," 72
Sophocles, 42
"Spot the Pussy," 109. *See also* pussy, as insult
Stoker, Bram, 17, 22, 29
Summers, Montague, 19

"Tale of Two Brothers," Egyptian, 33–54
thirsty dead, 22
Thompson, Stith, 35–36, 38
Tiger, Lionel, 100, 101
tomb-womb equation, 26
Totem and Taboo, 22–23
trident, significance of, 63, 69–71
Tylor, E. B., 128, 129, 135

Uchendu, Victor, 12

Vagina dentata, 25, 48, 67, 69
vampire, 16–32
Van Gennep, Arnold, 51, 101
Vanishing Hitchhiker, 80, 87–89
Vergote, Antoine, 4
Von Sydow, Carl Wilhelm, 33, 37, 38

Westermarck, Edward, 7
"Whale Tales," 108
wishful thinking, 29, 42, 45, 46
"Woody Check," 117

www.ingramcontent.com/pod-product-compliance
Lightning Source LLC
Chambersburg PA
CBHW030345240426
43661CB00052B/1745